Get Your Free Bonus Materials

Welcome to The Mature Singer's Guidebook!

PLEASE NOTE:

I have created online videos to assist
you in studying this material.

There will be points in the book where I will prompt you to find
a supplemental online lesson in your book members' area.

Please go to MatureSinger.com to access your free bonus content.

# THE MATURE SINGER'S

## GUIDEBOOK

Recapture, Revitalize, and Rejuvenate
Your Voice for a Lifetime of Singing

John Henny

JHVS Virtual, LLC
3857 Birch Street
Suite 3343
Newport Beach, CA 92660
United States
frontdesk@johnhenny.com
www.johnhenny.com

Although the author and publisher have made every effort to ensure that the information in this book was correct at press time, the author and publisher do not assume and hereby disclaim any liability to any party for any loss, damage, or disruption caused by errors or omissions, whether such errors or omissions result from negligence, accident, or any other cause.

The publisher and the author strongly recommend you consult with your ear, nose, and throat doctor (ENT) before beginning any voice program. The author is not a licensed healthcare care provider and represents that they have no expertise in diagnosing, examining, or treating vocal medical conditions of any kind, or in determining the effect of any specific exercise on a medical condition.

You should understand when participating in any vocal exercises, there is the possibility of physical injury. If you engage in these vocal exercises, you agree that you do so at your own risk, are voluntarily participating in these activities, assume all risk of injury to yourself, and agree to release and discharge the publisher and the author from any and all claims or causes of action, known or unknown, arising out of the contents of this book.

The publisher and the author advise you to take full responsibility for your safety and know your limits. Before practicing the skills described in this book, be sure that your voice is healthy enough for exercising and do not take risks beyond your level of experience, aptitude, training, and comfort level.

# CONTENTS

Welcome to The Mature Singer's Guidebook ....................................... vii

Chapter 1  My Vocal Crisis ................................................................1
Chapter 2  A Bit About Me ................................................................5
Chapter 3  Our Human Right to Sing ...............................................7
Chapter 4  How the Voice Works ....................................................10
Chapter 5  The Science of Aging .....................................................17
Chapter 6  The Aging Voice.............................................................21
Chapter 7  The Psychology of Singing and Aging ...................... 25
Chapter 8  Work Smarter AND Harder........................................ 30
Chapter 9  The HEROES System.....................................................32
Chapter 10  The 20-5-1- Rule........................................................... 36
Chapter 11  Hydration ..................................................................... 40
Chapter 12  Exercise......................................................................... 46
Chapter 13  Strengthening Exercises ...............................................51
Chapter 14  SOVT Exercises ............................................................59
Chapter 15  Range ............................................................................63
Chapter 16  Range Exercises............................................................67
Chapter 17  Optimize .......................................................................70
Chapter 18  Optimize Exercises .......................................................76
Chapter 19  Energy............................................................................ 80
Chapter 20  Vibrato Exercises.......................................................... 84

Chapter 21  Body Work ........................................................ 86

Chapter 22  Emotional Expression.................................... 88

Chapter 23  Mindfulness and Meditation....................... 92

Chapter 24  SING! ............................................................. 97

Chapter 25  Health Benefits ............................................ 100

Chapter 26  Voice Doctors ............................................... 103

Chapter 27  Real Life Experiences................................... 106

Chapter 28  Next Steps..................................................... 110

Chapter 29  Resources....................................................... 112

Acknowledgments............................................................. 115

What Did You Think?....................................................... 117

About the Author ............................................................. 118

Also by John Henny .......................................................... 119

# WELCOME TO THE MATURE SINGER'S GUIDEBOOK

Your voice is meant to last a lifetime. My job as a voice teacher is to help ensure it does.

This guidebook is based on the latest research and cutting-edge techniques to keep your voice healthy, flexible, and vital in your 50s, 60s, 70s, and beyond.

Or, if you are just starting your singing journey, this guide will show you how to find and stay on the path of continuous vocal health.

## The Aging Voice

Like the rest of our bodies, our voices change over time. As we age, physiological transformations occur within our vocal mechanism. Our vocal cords lose elasticity and lubrication, the muscles surrounding our larynx weaken, and our lung capacity diminishes.

These changes can impact our voice's range, strength, and quality, posing unique challenges to seasoned singers or those just starting their vocal journey.

However, while age may bring changes, it also brings richness, depth, and a wealth of experiences to our voices. It is crucial, therefore, to address the unique needs of the aging voice and allow it to continue to be an instrument for expression, emotion, and connection.

## Your Guidebook

This guidebook will introduce you to my HEROES System—a holistic approach focusing on vocal health and rejuvenation. Each component of this method addresses a vital aspect of singing and offers insights and strategies to revitalize and maintain your singing voice.

Whether you are a professional singer, a choral enthusiast, or someone who simply finds joy in singing, this guide offers practical, actionable strategies to enhance your vocal longevity and resilience.

Remember, age is not a barrier; it's a gateway to deeper, more meaningful musical expression. Welcome to your journey to a timeless voice!

## Using This Book

This guidebook has two main goals: first, to give you a working knowledge of your voice as it ages and the challenges we older singers must contend with, and second, to provide you with practical exercises to strengthen your instrument.

While this guidebook can be used by singers at any level, beginners may want an additional resource, which is why I have created an online bonus section with video and audio versions of the exercises and extra materials.

Go to maturesinger.com to access your free content or use the QR code below:

I have also arranged for you to have free access to a digital copy of my bestselling book, *Beginning Singing*.

Go here to access your copy: beginningsinging.com

I am giving you these resources for free because I want you to be successful. I know it takes time to trust someone before making further purchases from them, and I want to remove any barrier to your success.

I recommend reading through this guidebook once and then returning to the chapters and exercises that most interest you.

I would love to know how this guidebook has worked for you or any other feedback you may have. Please feel free to reach out to frontdesk@johnhenny.com with your thoughts.

## CHAPTER ONE

# My Vocal Crisis

already knew what she would say next, but it didn't make it any easier.

"John, you have a benign essential vocal tremor."

And there it was. My voice, the one thing that had taken me around the world and allowed me to work with some of my musical heroes, was failing me.

It is difficult to pinpoint the cause of a vocal tremor, but there is no mistaking its effects. The signals from my brain to my vocal cords were misfiring, creating a rhythmic pulsing or shaking sound.

And it wasn't just an issue with the pulsing; it created problems with balance throughout my vocal instrument. As my body tried to compensate for the tremor, tension and squeezing started to work their way into my singing and vocalizing.

At first, I thought it was vocal fatigue or perhaps a side-effect from recent weight loss.

But it didn't go away.

My voice became rougher, weaker, strained. And with a vocal tremor, there is no known cure.

I had just turned sixty, and my first age-related challenge was bringing me to my vocal knees. While current medical science is unable to link a vocal tremor to a known underlying condition, it tends to happen to people in their fifties and sixties. My tremor was right on time.

As I ended the call, I sat stunned. And then the tears came. My voice, my career, my identity, my sense of worth in this mass of humanity all shattered in some way or another.

I allowed myself fifteen minutes of mourning, then took a deep breath and made a vow. From that point forward, I would consider this tremor a gift from the vocal gods. A blessing that would push me deeper into voice than I had ever gone.

And perhaps I would emerge from this beautiful struggle with additional ways to help others who have experienced voice loss.

This book is part of what has emerged.

There is a lot of self-imposed pressure when you are a voice teacher. Every note you sing is being judged in some way by the public and (sometimes even more harshly) by your peers.

As my vocal issues started, my confidence was shaken. I had done a vocal demonstration on a YouTube video and an anonymous person commented that while I appeared to know a lot about singing, I should never sing because my voice was terrible.

I tried to make a lighthearted joke about the comment on my YouTube page, only to be taunted by another voice teacher:

"You should record really high songs like Steve Perry and Bruno Mars and post those."

This voice teacher knew that my upper range was falling apart, and that I could not sing anything close to those songs in my current condition. Instead of offering support, they decided to publicly mock me.

As a voice teacher, I knew what I should do—or at least thought I did.

The old adage says, "He who represents himself has a fool for a client."

And I was that fool.

I tried to remove the tension I felt, and my voice shook more. I tried to stabilize my voice, and it became strained and effortful. I was stuck.

Getting that painful diagnosis was life-changing in a wonderful way. I began working with Kerrie Obert, one of the top voice researchers and speech-language pathologists (as well as a fantastic voice teacher).

Kerrie worked my voice in different ways than my previous teachers (who had dealt with a younger and better-functioning instrument).

She showed me that my relationship with my voice had to change. I had to change not only how I used my voice but also how I thought of and took care of it.

I could no longer take long breaks from singing, studying, and practicing and expect my voice to be there. I was now in the battle against time.

Getting older is a funny thing. We all know we will be a senior citizen someday (if we are able to stay above ground), but we never truly think it's going to happen to us. Such is the illusion of permanence.

This went far beyond my annoyance at being offered my first senior discount at a fast-food restaurant—this was now a real consequence of the ticking clock.

With Kerrie, I worked to bring back elasticity and function to my vocal cords while eliminating the excess tension that my nervous system had clung to.

I reduced (and practically eliminated) the tremor through a series of exercises that strengthened the muscles of my vocal tract and tongue, giving my nervous system a new anchor against the shaking.

At first, little seemed to be happening. But at the six-month mark, I could sustain notes without a tremor, and my upper range started returning.

My excitement pushed me to study more about the voice (I was already a bit of a voice science geek to begin with) and to understand how to help others.

It turns out these exercises and approaches were not limited to those suffering from a tremor—they could help everyone dealing with age-related voice issues.

And if your voice is still working great at fifty, this could help your voice stay that way for decades.

I now have a profound sense of gratitude for my tremor and for being led to the work of Kerrie Obert. I'm thrilled to share these lessons with you.

## CHAPTER TWO

# A Bit About Me

'm an unlikely voice teacher, or at least my younger self would have thought so. I began my musical journey as a drummer because I was convinced I couldn't sing. But even as I began to make my living playing the drums, the desire to sing never left me.

I was not blessed with a natural ability; I had to work for every bit of vocal improvement. I didn't try in earnest until my twenties when a roommate mentioned that he was studying voice.

As luck would have it, I worked with one of the legendary voice teachers in Los Angeles, Seth Riggs, who was also teaching Stevie Wonder, Michael Jackson, and Prince.

I was in some pretty good company!

I certainly struggled in the beginning, but with consistent lessons and diligent study, I became a lead singer and even had an independent record deal at one time. Alas, a couple of hits on college radio in the 90s was as far as that went.

In between gigs and recording sessions, I started to help some friends with their voices and found my calling. I became completely fascinated with the voice and began teaching full-time. I even started showing others how to teach and created one of the first online voice teacher training programs.

I became a columnist for Backstage Magazine, was a guest lecturer at USC and the Paul McCartney Liverpool Institute of the Arts (as a Beatles fan, this was a particular high point), and gave masterclasses on the voice throughout Europe, Japan, and Australia. My podcast, *The Intelligent Vocalist*, has tens of thousands of listeners worldwide. My four previous books have all become Amazon bestsellers.

I have now worked with thousands of singers and teachers around the world. It has been my honor and pleasure to work with music superstars and Grammy winners, as well as passionate amateurs.

As I reached the age of sixty (wait, this aging thing is really happening?), I realized my instrument was changing—being an older singer was no longer theoretical for me. The before-mentioned vocal tremor created even more urgency to restore and preserve my voice.

I also saw another career path emerge to help others regain what time is trying to take from them. With the right system, we can slow down the clock and reclaim our birthright to express ourselves with the vibrations of singing.

This book is the culmination of my vocal past and present.

Four decades of singing and over thirty years of teaching are in these pages, as well as the knowledge of my brilliant vocal peers and teachers.

It is my hope this book helps you reconnect, regain, and reclaim your voice.

## CHAPTER THREE

# Our Human Right to Sing

The young British musician, composer, and vocalist Jacob Collier is a once-in-a-generation talent.

One of the highlights of Jacob's concerts is when he gets the audience to sing, but not in the typical way of a call-and-response or singing along with the chorus.

Jacob breaks the audience into different sections and utilizes them as a live choir, each section changing their part as Jacob moves his hands up and down.

The result is an absolute work of beauty, yet Jacob doesn't make a sound. With no prior practice or preparation, the audience creates stunningly complex choral music.

For the audience, it is a transcendent moment as the vibrations of their combined voices and emotions reverberate all around them.

Singing puts us in touch with something deeper in our core and communicates with others in emotionally complex ways that the spoken word cannot. Some theorize that the first language of early humans was a type of singing that expressed and communicated emotion.

The theory of "musilanguage" is that early human communication had characteristics of both music and language, blending elements like melody, rhythm, and expressive intonation with more structured, symbolic aspects typical of language. Over time, these two systems are thought to have diverged into the distinct forms of music and language we recognize today.

Singing goes back to our earliest beginnings and is hard-wired within us. The cooing of a baby is singing, and older children will sing constantly with no need for encouragement.

One of my missions to get people to sing, no matter their technical level. It's hard to stay in a poor mood or to be stressed when you are singing. It creates profound changes in the body and mind.

The creation of a professional class of singers is a gift to humanity. To listen to talented and skilled individuals perform music at high levels is a fantastic way to spend time. But the downside to being exposed to these great vocalists is that people who can't measure up to this level often think they cannot sing and stop doing it. The same people who sang as children have let a fantastic resource of physical and mental health drop from their lives.

This idea of an entry-level bar also causes older singers to quit or reduce their amount of singing.

I don't want this for you.

Yes, the challenges of singing can increase as we age, but in no way should that mean we stop. If you follow the guidelines in this book and incorporate the concepts into a daily practice routine, you can maintain your birthright to sing.

It is always more enjoyable to perform an activity when it has a sense of ease and flow. My goal is to give you back more of the ease and flow you felt when you were younger while honoring the instrument you have now (and will have in the future).

Johnny Cash did some of his most acclaimed work in the later part of his life. Just before his death at the age of 71, and dealing with major health issues, Johnny released his cover of the song "Hurt," composed by Trent Reznor. The age and pathos in Johnny's voice completely eclipsed the original version for many listeners. The accompanying video won a Grammy, and the New Music Express named it the best music video of all time.

If Johnny had recorded this song as a younger man, it would have been fine, but nowhere near as emotionally devastating as the 70-year-old Johnny gave us.

Such is the impact of the older artist.

One of my clients performs with a famous legacy rock band from the 70s. As my student enters his mid-sixties, he performs material recorded fifty years ago by the original vocalist, who was then in his twenties.

The keys and range of these songs are incredibly challenging (even for a young singer), yet my client nails these songs (in the original keys) nightly on long, rigorous tours.

He feels his voice has never been stronger.

His dedication to his instrument, health, and practice is exemplary, but it shows us the possibilities.

No matter your age today, there is so much singing ahead for you.

CHAPTER FOUR

# How the Voice Works

Before we delve deeper into the voice and aging, let's start with a quick primer on how the voice works. This will be helpful as we begin to work with our instrument later in the book.

The human voice can be viewed as a rather simple instrument. You send air to the vocal cords, creating sound waves that are enhanced by the vocal tract (your throat and mouth), which then pass through your lips and out to the world.

But a deeper look reveals an instrument of incredible complexity.

When we sing, our breathing goes from a mostly passive activity to a vibrant and energized one. We need to control the flow of air by keeping the muscles of inspiration and exhalation in balanced opposition. The vocal cords change their tension, thickness, and length to create a wide range of pitches.

(Note: the proper name for the vocal cords is *vocal folds*, or simply *folds*. I will be using these terms for the remainder of the book. Your vocal folds are located near the bottom of your thyroid cartilage, which is often called the Adam's apple, and lie horizontally over your trachea or windpipe and open when inhaling and close when making sound).

The vocal folds also need to create different levels of resistance to the airflow. Essentially, the longer the folds stay closed against the air, the more intense or louder the sound waves will be.

The vocal tract, including the throat, mouth, soft palate, tongue, and lips then need to coordinate to bring out the intended properties of the sound waves. As you move the various parts of your vocal tract, you will enhance certain parts of the sound waves and reduce or eliminate others. This filtering gives us our tone and vowels.

Each note requires changes of airflow, vocal fold tension and resistance, and acoustic vocal tract tunings, and we need to negotiate these changes with balance and skill to avoid the dreaded vocal break, where the voice starts to strain or crack.

There is a wide array of muscles and ligaments involved in the process. Indeed, the whole body is involved, from pitch-making and resonance to the posture we hold to keep the entire mechanism in a dynamic state.

I want you to think of singing not as something that happens in the throat but as something that encompasses your full body, spirit, and energy. It is this complex, dynamic system that makes singing so wonderful for us older adults.

The daily act of exercising this instrument has enormous health advantages, both physical and mental. But as we age, our physical voice will undergo changes, which means the way we interact with it will need to change as well.

What worked at age thirty will likely not work today, and what works today may not work five years from now. It is an ever-changing, ever-evolving process that is a beautiful part of maintaining this instrument.

## Non-Linear

The voice is a non-linear system, which means that small changes in one part of the process will yield significant changes in the output. This creates confusion for the singer as it feels like the voice jumps from one extreme to another (i.e., moving from weak and breathy to suddenly strained and shouty).

The changes brought by aging also contribute to these non-linear shifts. We want to be careful to avoid overcorrecting or allowing the body to adapt to these changes in vocally unhealthy ways.

In my case, the onset of my vocal tremor created changes in the singing mechanism that manifested wildly shifting results, and my initial attempts to correct the voice created additional issues.

As you practice and work the voice, you will experience some of these variations. I urge you not to get frustrated; rather, I encourage you to accept that this is the instrument you have been given. The beautiful part is you are the only person among billions with your particular voice.

The non-linear aspect of your vocal system requires patience and non-judgment. Take your time and allow your voice to create new balances and relationships. As your coordination and muscles strengthen, your voice will certainly improve.

## The Vocal Folds

In this book, I encourage you to work harder and strengthen muscles associated with singing—but this effort and strengthening does NOT happen at the vocal folds.

The vocal folds are the one part of the body where we do not want to feel tension or an extreme increase in effort. The surface level of the folds needs to vibrate, which means this softer tissue can be damaged with over-stress and high-impact collisions.

The vocal folds vibrate hundreds of times a second while singing (and in excess of 1,000 for extreme high notes). Compare this to the wings of hummingbirds which flap at a mere fifty to eighty times per second.

This stunningly fast process of opening and closing needs to be efficient and balanced to avoid damage to the surface of the folds.

## The Vocal Tract

Without your vocal tract, the sound coming from your vocal folds would be closer to a quacking duck than a human voice. The tube comprising of your throat and mouth is the magic part of the process that turns this buzzing little reed into a recognizable voice.

The vocal tract also gives us power, tone, clarity, and language. I argue that this tube is the most important part of our voice.

The vocal tract starts just above the folds and continues up the throat, past the root of the tongue, through the mouth, and finally to the lips.

Note: the nasal cavity can be opened to join the system but it will give us a nasal sound, which is not always desired. For voiced consonants such as M and N, however, the nasal cavity is an active resonator.

What makes the vocal tract such an amazing part of our instrument is that it is highly flexible and has several elements that can be adjusted for different results. For instance, the height of your larynx (or voice box) can move up and down, as can your soft palate.

Your jaw can drop and your lips can round, spread, or pucker. Your throat can be wider or more compressed. Your tongue (which is made up of multiple independent muscles) can move forward, back, up, and down simultaneously!

Every one of these movements affects not just the sound of your voice but also your vocal balance and ability to sing certain notes.

The vocal tract is also where we can experience age-related issues that go unnoticed. We often blame problems on our breath support or vocal folds, but often the issue can be solved by adjustments in the vocal tract since weakness in the throat and tongue muscles can impact our voice greatly.

When I worked with Kerrie Obert to control my vocal tremor, one of the first things we did was a series of exercises to strengthen the vocal folds and, more importantly, my vocal tract. Once I strengthened my vocal tract and tongue, I was able to anchor and control the tremor without squeezing at the folds.

But it's not just a greater ability to anchor the voice that is the magic of your vocal tract—it's the acoustics!

## Vocal Acoustics

This subject is a hot topic with researchers, and I have an in-depth course called *The New Science of Singing* where I discuss and teach vocal acoustics. It is a passion of mine.

The simple summary of vocal acoustics is the sound waves initiated by your vocal folds are not strong enough for communication and singing. They also do not impart recognizable vowel sounds. The work of enhancing the vibration into words and tones that can be heard over an orchestra belongs to the amazing vocal tract.

This tract is analogous to a recording studio mixing board. In the studio, the sound engineer can move levers and dials to bring out different parts of the recorded music, making some tracks and frequencies louder and others softer or inaudible. Likewise, the movement of the vocal tract brings out certain parts of the sound wave while attenuating or diminishing others. The vocal tract has movable resonances that amplify parts of the sound wave that are within their value.

Note: Resonances are natural acoustic boosts within an acoustic space, such as a theatre, parking garage, recording booth, or the vocal tract. Every acoustic space has different resonances, depending on the size and shape. That's why engineers need to adjust the mix to each venue an artist performs in.

For instance, if a resonance has a value of 600 vibrations per second (or hertz), then parts (or partials) of the sound wave vibrating at or near 600 hertz will get more excited and become louder. As the resonance moves away from the partials of the sound wave, their energy will diminish.

In the vocal tract, if our resonances are aligned correctly, we will have optimal tone and balance throughout our range. The problem is our nervous system is used to certain relationships of the resonances and sound waves, primarily the ones used in speech.

When we attempt to sing higher, our nervous system attempts to maintain these relationships. As we go even higher, the sound wave changes; therefore, the resonance needs to change to create new relationships, otherwise we will experience the dreaded vocal break where we either shout or let go and crack to a weak sound.

The best way to create these new tunings of resonance is through vowel modification. This allows us to move smoothly from our lower to upper registers, which is often referred to as registration.

Vowels need to shift as we ascend through our range. While this is not specific to the older voice, this is a vital concept all singers should know and we will explore these methods further within this book.

In addition, you can find out more about vowel tuning and registration in my book *Beginning Singing*, which is available as a free digital download here. beginningsinging.com

Now that we have the basics, let's look closer at how aging affects us and our vocal instrument.

## CHAPTER FIVE

# The Science of Aging

Aging is a process that has similar effects but is unique to each of us. From the moment of conception, we embark on a journey of aging, and while the first part is associated with growth and potential, the latter part can carry a stigma of decline.

While science is actively working to unlock the secrets of aging to reverse some of its effects, there is much we can currently do to stay healthy in our later years. A certain amount of this process is genetic, just like the unique vocal equipment you were born with.

Individual genetics influence the aging process in various ways. Our genes regulate key cellular processes such as replication, repair, and apoptosis, which affects how quickly cells age as well as their ability to repair damage.

Some people possess "longevity genes" that are more prevalent in those who live to an exceptionally old age, offering protective effects against common age-related diseases or conferring greater cellular resilience.

The body's ability to handle oxidative stress, caused by free radicals, is also partially determined by genetics. Some individuals may have a higher natural antioxidant capacity, which protects cells from damage and slows the aging process. Our organs will age differently depending on hormone regulation. Even our chromosomes will have variations in what time does to us.

While genetics play a vital role in aging, it's crucial to remember that they are not the sole determinant. Lifestyle factors and environmental exposures also significantly contribute to how we age. Therefore, a combination of favorable genetics and healthy lifestyle choices can optimize the aging process.

It has been said that genetics are the dynamite but lifestyle is the match. If we dedicate ourselves to vocal, physical, and mental health, we can create a more positive outcome despite our genetics.

In terms of the voice, we all have genetic limitations as to what our voice can do at each stage of our lives. But it is rarely genetics alone that creates our current limitations. It is our habits, lifestyle, regimens, techniques, and mindset that are the real obstacles.

## The Benefits of Aging

I have found that even with the challenge of a vocal tremor, my enjoyment of singing—and indeed, even my levels of general happiness—have increased as I get older. And I am not alone. Many older adults report greater life satisfaction and happiness, underpinned by a deepened emotional resilience. This period of life brings a wealth of experiences that contribute to greater wisdom and perspective.

Having navigated diverse life situations, older adults tend to have well-developed coping mechanisms, can view problems from multiple perspectives, and typically adopt a more balanced approach to life's challenges.

Emotional control and self-regulation also tend to improve with age. Older adults often demonstrate an enhanced ability to regulate their emotions and react to negative events with greater composure, contributing to overall emotional stability.

While it is true that some cognitive abilities decline as we get older, certain cognitive faculties like vocabulary and specific types of memory often remain stable or even improve over time.

Socially, aging is associated with stronger, more meaningful relationships. The depth of experience allows older adults to cultivate richer interpersonal connections, which often results in increased altruism and volunteerism.

Many older adults find personal fulfillment and a sense of purpose in contributing positively to their communities through volunteer work. The rich life experiences and enhanced communication skills that come with age also mean that older individuals are often well-positioned to offer valuable advice, empathy, and support to others.

From a health and lifestyle perspective, many older adults become more conscious of their choices, leading to improved nutritional choices and increased physical activity. This greater focus on health is invaluable for the vocal instrument, as the voice reflects your general level of health.

The process of aging should not be viewed solely in terms of decline. Instead, it's a period filled with opportunities for growth, learning, and active contribution. This makes our older years one of the best times in life to focus on singing. Not only are we often in a better place mentally to commit to and express ourselves with music, but the act of singing also provides great benefits for older adults.

However, there are some physical vocal challenges you will likely have to contend with. Let's dive into those now.

## CHAPTER SIX

# The Aging Voice

The process of growing older will give us several distinctively different voices throughout our lifetime. As a small child, the vocal folds and vocal tract are relatively small, giving us higher voices. Our voice deepens slightly as we become older children, and then the big vocal event arrives: puberty.

In the typical female voice (voices not influenced by testosterone), the larynx (voice box) widens and the vocal folds become longer. Vocal folds that are influenced by testosterone lengthen substantially, causing the Adam's apple protrusion. The pitch of the voice drops, sometimes dramatically.

After a rocky post-puberty restart (especially for voices that deepen dramatically), the voice matures into the vibrant, flexible voice of the young adult. This is the sound of the pop singer, the musical theatre ingenue, or the high-flying rock star.

Then comes the older adult. In your thirties, the voice continues to strengthen, perhaps losing a little flexibility but gaining robustness and richness. Some say this is the peak of the voice.

Middle age can bring some less-than-desirable changes. Just as the body naturally softens and weakens, the voice can lose some of its strength and range. Perimenopause can start to show in a singer's voice as soon as the late thirties.

By our fifties, time is no longer on our side, and a number of changes can start to develop, including:

Less Vocal Fold Elasticity: Younger vocal folds are more elastic, which allows for a greater range of pitch and volume. With age, the vocal folds and surrounding tissues lose a degree of elasticity, often leading to a decrease in overall range.

Atrophy: As we age, the muscles of the vocal folds can atrophy or become thinner, leading to a weaker, breathier voice.

Laryngeal Cartilages Calcification: The cartilages of the larynx (voice box) may calcify and stiffen over time, which can limit the motion of the vocal folds and larynx during speech and singing.

Changes in Respiratory System: The respiratory system, which provides the power for the voice, can weaken with age. This can lead to reduced lung capacity and breath control, affecting sustained notes and the ability to project the voice.

Menopause: In women, menopause can lead to hormonal changes that may cause the voice to become deeper and less flexible.

Andropause: Men experience a gradual decrease in testosterone levels, which can lead to changes in voice pitch and quality.

There may also be health issues and medications that affect the voice and hydration levels, an essential concept that I will explain later. Lifestyle changes such as retirement may mean you are using your voice less, which can contribute to weakening and atrophy.

While we can never entirely stop the vocal aging process, the good news is we can slow it down and even recover a great deal of our vocal abilities. The irony is that our instrument wants to become less expressive just as we have more experience and, therefore, more to express musically.

Our brains even communicate on a higher level as we age. Some studies suggest that older adults can use both hemispheres of the brain for tasks that younger adults only use one side for, which may lead to better problem-solving abilities. All of these contribute to artistic maturity and a greater ability to connect with an audience. It is so important to help older singers reclaim their voices.

Here's another bit of truth: as an older singer, you will have to work harder to keep your voice working. I'm not talking about marathon practice sessions, but you will need to be consistent in your practice and application.

The act of singing itself will require more energy and engagement than when you were twenty-five. I will show you some of my favorite exercises to build strength and energy and how to reignite vitality in your singing. The "use it or lose it" mentality certainly applies to the voice, and I have two secret weapons to help you fight against the "lose it" part.

My HEROES System will give you a framework for vocal health and reawakening.

And my 20-5-1 Rule will keep you on track and consistently improving.

By utilizing the HEROES method and the 20-5-1 framework, your voice can improve and even flourish in the years to come.

Singing is our human birthright, and it is my life's work to keep everyone singing for as long as they wish. Are you ready to discover your beautifully mature, most expressive voice?

Then let's go!

## CHAPTER SEVEN

# The Psychology of Singing and Aging

The connection between the mind and voice is powerful when we are singing. We do not have keys to press or strings to pluck, but rather an instrument of imperfect feedback.

We cannot see the voice, and our connections to the sensations of singing can be a bit mysterious and blurry. It is the quality of our thoughts that directly controls this instrument—thoughts not just of technique, but also mindset and emotion.

As we age and experience physical changes with the voice, we often experience mental shifts. These shifts can directly impact our relationship with our instrument and even our ability to sing.

Experienced singers have a strong relationship with their voices and a certain level of identity and self-perception. As the voice undergoes age-related changes, there can be frustration and even a sense of mourning as our youthful voice is replaced.

I know I went through a period of being afraid that people would judge me for my vocal tremor. I was terrified that I would be viewed as having less skill as a voice teacher, especially when compared to younger voices.

It was in the moment of finally being diagnosed that I clearly understood what was happening with my voice, and I could accept the new reality and challenge.

One of the hardest parts about my changing voice were the changes in my confidence levels. The voice is guided by thought rather than the direct physical contact of other instruments, which have tangible frets or keys to press. If we have doubt or fear before singing a note, the results are likely to be different from what we intend.

Aging can throw off our necessary confidence, especially if we are holding on to the voice of our youth or stressing over new challenges. By starting a regimen of specific exercises for the older voice, you can develop a new relationship with your instrument and find confidence in your new vocal skills.

As you work with your voice—whether in lessons, online courses, or the practice room—you will likely need to make adjustments. I will show you how to make these shifts in your exercise and practice routines to work with your current voice.

## Accepting and Embracing the Aging Voice

The first step is understanding that vocal changes are a natural part of aging. Accepting these changes can help you adapt to the new vocal reality. Again, don't judge your current voice against the voice that was. The best approach is to be clear and honest with yourself and to eliminate comparing your voice to others.

Our voices are ultimately incomparable; that's the beauty of singing. Keep reminding yourself to fall in love with your instrument every day. The ability to sing at any level is precious, and as long as we are breathing and able to make sound, we can improve. Keep yourself open to new possibilities and means of expression.

Aging can open up new musical avenues better suited to the mature voice, particularly if the material emphasizes storytelling and emotion over vocal acrobatics.

With age also comes emotional depth and experience, and focusing on emotional expression in singing can be fulfilling and can make performances more impactful. I will dedicate a chapter to this later in the book.

## Psychological Benefits of Singing in Older Age

Singing not only enhances our physical health but also significantly improves brain and psychological health. The act of singing has been shown to release endorphins, reduce stress, and improve mood. This has a positive impact on our emotional well-being and overall mood.

Singing offers a range of direct cognitive benefits beyond the emotional and psychological uplift it provides. It exercises the brain in various ways, improving memory and cognitive functions.

When singing, the brain is tasked with learning lyrics and melodies, which requires complex memorization processes. This mental exercise strengthens neural connections, enhancing short-term and long-term memory capabilities. Remembering lyrics and associating them with melodies activates various parts of the brain, including those responsible for auditory processing, language, and memory storage.

Singing involves the coordination of multiple brain functions. It requires integrating language skills for understanding and producing lyrics, auditory skills for pitch recognition and vocalization, and motor skills for controlling the vocal folds and breathing. This multitasking nature of singing helps to improve overall cognitive function, making the brain more agile and efficient.

The rhythmic and repetitive aspects of singing also contribute to cognitive health. Engaging regularly with rhythm and melody can enhance pattern recognition skills, which are fundamental in various cognitive tasks. Furthermore, the emotional connection formed while singing can lead to deeper engagement with the material, further strengthening cognitive pathways.

Regular singing practice can encourage the brain to create new pathways and strengthen existing ones, improving brain function and resilience against cognitive decline.

The cognitive benefits of singing are multifaceted and significant. Regularly engaging in singing improves abilities, from memory and attention, to complex problem-solving skills, while also enjoying the emotional and social benefits of singing.

## Case Studies and Examples

Drawing upon examples from well-known aging singers can provide inspiration and insight. Many have adapted their styles and continued to have successful careers, often finding deeper artistic satisfaction in their mature voices.

In working and conversing with older singers, I find the majority welcome this new stage of their singing life and find the trade-off of experience and emotional connection for youth to be musically worthwhile. Here are just a few comments I have received from mature singers.

"Singing is a more intense, full-body experience!"

"I have become much more emotional and connected to songs I want to perform."

"Singing has grown deeper and more meaningful."

I find it helpful to remember that the past no longer exists except in memory. The future only resides in our fantasies. Our only reality is this moment.

The only voice you have is in this moment as well.

By fully embracing the singer you are right now, you can maintain the joy of singing, and we can work our way to being even better tomorrow.

# Work Smarter AND Harder

The following may be slightly controversial, especially considering the oft-sought ideal of singing with complete relaxation and ease. Once again, I credit my work with Kerrie Obert for bringing these concepts into focus for me.

As I began to struggle with my vocal tremor, my body tried to steady the unintended pulsing in my folds with excess tension. As my body did this, my voice-teacher mind would stop and try to remove the tension by attempting to release and let go of the excess effort.

The result was an increase in the tremor, a weakening of power, a degradation of tone, and a slowing of my vibrato. Even my ability to match pitch was becoming impacted.

This crisis in my singing led me to accept a new and possibly controversial approach.

My aging nerves no longer fired as rapidly to my voice, and this slowing also recruited fewer muscle fibers. The answer was not to use less muscle but to involve more!

To increase the speed of neural conduction, we need to increase the contraction of the body parts we are engaging. If you are an experienced singer starting to face age-related changes, you will likely need to change your approach. What has worked in the past will not serve your voice in the upcoming years.

Again, the connection between the mind and voice is critical, and this connection is getting slower. By employing the right approaches and strategically engaging more muscle fiber in the right parts of the instrument, you can discover a vocal fountain of youth.

I have had clients go from a slow, wide vocal wobble to a spinning, youthful vibrato by employing more effort, not by reducing it.

And this extra work is fun! You will feel a new connection and vitality in your voice.

The extra energy will infuse your body and emotional communication, and this ever-unfolding challenge is a blessing to all who have claimed our birthright to sing.

Although you now have a different instrument, I work with clients who feel they sing better now than in their youth. The challenges of the older voice have inspired and motivated them to keep their instrument working at a high level.

In the next chapter, we will look at my HEROES System and how it can be a framework to take your voice into your most golden years.

## CHAPTER NINE

# The HEROES System

As I worked against my uncurable vocal tremor, I started to create frameworks to keep me focused and moving forward in the healthiest and most efficient ways possible. Each day, I am working to slow the progression of this condition.

Utilizing the HEROES System, I am extending my singing life by at least a decade or more. The HEROES System focuses on six essential elements of the older singer's vocal health and singing ability.

I use this framework every day for vocal improvement, and we will look at each element in-depth in the following chapters. I will also give you my best recommendations on how to apply this to your daily life and practice.

As a reader of this book, you have access to free supplemental materials, including audio versions of the vocal exercises.

Go to maturesinger.com to access your bonus materials.

By using HEROES on a consistent basis, you can help minimize the changes in your voice.

The six pillars of the HEROES System are:

- Hydration
- Exercise
- Range
- Optimize
- Energy
- Sing

Let's get a quick overview:

## Hydration: The Vocal Lifeline

Hydration is not just about drinking water; it's about understanding how fluids interact with your vocal folds. The mucous membrane covering the vocal folds needs constant hydration to vibrate efficiently. The folds also require constant hydration at the cellular level, which calls for increased diligence as we age.

I'll introduce you to hydration strategies beyond the usual eight-glasses-a-day rule, including how different beverages affect your vocal folds and how to use humidifiers and nebulizers effectively, especially in drier climates or seasons.

## Exercise: Building the Voice

As discussed in the previous chapter, we must harness additional muscle activity as our voice ages, which necessitates a different approach to working our voice. It's important to engage not just our breathing and vocal folds but also our tongue and muscles of the vocal tract.

Some of the approaches to vocal exercises will likely be new to you. I will explain the how and why behind each exercise so you can focus on both function and desired results.

## Range: Embracing Change and Adaptation

Your vocal range will change with age, but this isn't necessarily a limitation. I'll teach you how to embrace and adapt to these changes. We'll focus on exercises that help you explore the new characteristics of your voice, such as the rich, resonant tones that come with maturity.

We'll also look at techniques for maintaining your upper range and even reclaiming some of the notes you may have lost.

## Optimize: Maximum Efficiency

While we must work harder as older singers, we still want to maximize our vocal balance and efficiency. We will look at developing and maintaining smooth registration, which will eliminate strain and vocal breaks.

We will also delve into the near-magical power of resonance. I will give you strategies to get the maximum energy and tone from your voice without overworking it.

## Energy: The Intersection of Physical and Mental Vitality

Energy management is crucial for older singers. It's not just about physical energy; mental and emotional health also play a significant role in vocal performance.

This section will cover techniques to improve your focus and emotional well-being, such as mindfulness practices and mental exercises to enhance your connection with music. I'll also explore strategies to help you find new dimensions of emotional connection and expression in your singing.

## Sing: Let's Do This!

Finally, we come to the core of it all: the practical aspects of singing with an aging voice. Singing is a fantastic gift to yourself, but its true power comes from sharing. We will look at the social benefits of singing and how it can increase your mental and physical well-being.

## The HEROES Journey: Integrating the System into Your Life

By the end of this book, you'll have a comprehensive understanding of the HEROES System and how to apply it to extend and enrich your singing life. Each element works in concert to support your voice, helping you maintain and enhance your vocal abilities as you age.

By using the six pillars as a daily framework, you can recapture and rebuild a dynamic voice for your singing lifetime.

There is a commitment needed from you, but it is not extreme. If you can dedicate twenty minutes daily to these concepts, you will experience a shift in your singing and overall vocal health.

Yes, your voice is different from the one you had at 25, but it is no less important or expressive. Your range will likely diminish slightly, but there will be new levels of richness—and perhaps an extended range in the lower notes.

You CAN change your voice, and the HEROES System is the best way to do this.

CHAPTER TEN

# The 20-5-1- Rule

To improve and build the voice, consistent effort and application is essential. It does us little good to do two hours of practice one day a week. In fact, for most older singers this could be a strain on the voice.

There is a minimum amount of practice you will want to do, but this minimum will help create massive change.

For this, I use my 20-5-1 rule as a guide:

- Twenty minutes a day
- Five days a week
- No more than one week off in a three month period.

Less than seven hours a month to allow you to keep singing, It's a fantastic return on investment!

## Practicing

Let's talk about practicing. The key is not how much time is spent, but rather *how* it is spent. We want these twenty minutes to give us maximum impact.

I recommend creating a dedicated practice area. It doesn't need to be large but should feel comfortable and inspiring. For example, I purchased a vocal booth that is four-by-six feet wide and seven feet tall, which gives me more than enough space for myself and my keyboard. I can practice whenever I want without disturbing anyone. It's an investment but well worth it for me.

You don't need a vocal booth, just a functional space.

In my singing space, I keep various vocalizing straws, a nebulizer (more on these later), and a small device that is my secret weapon. It's a bit of technology that has been around for over a thousand years: an hourglass or sand timer.

I have a twenty-minute hourglass that I turn over at the start of each practice session. The physical ritual of doing this cues my mind and body to get ready to work. Also, watching the sand fall gives a sense of urgency, which helps keep me focused on the task at hand.

Another essential part of practicing is working on the right things for YOUR voice.

While I am not able to personally diagnose your voice and prescribe the appropriate exercises, the HEROES System will help you create a powerful exercise routine.

I recommend leaving your phone in another room, or if you use it to look up lyrics or record yourself for analysis (which I highly recommend), put it on "do not disturb." These twenty minutes are a sacred gift to yourself and your voice.

Practices like this, five days a week will give you consistency and create a growing wave of improvement and motivation.

Not taking more than one week off is a BIG part of the rule. Because part of aging is the weakening and atrophying of our muscles, physical exercise becomes increasingly vital to our health. As I type this, I have a timer next to me that goes off at twenty-five-minute intervals to remind me to get up, walk, and stretch. As they say, sitting is the new smoking.

The muscles of your voice are no different. An amazingly complex system of muscles, ligaments, and tissues are involved in the act of singing. Singing is incredibly physical in a way that's different from other instruments such as guitar or piano.

If we take more than a week off from our consistent vocal practice, we invite the creeping nemesis of atrophy into our voice. The vocal folds need strength, flexibility, and the optimal alignment of the edges, which is essential to creating rich, robust sound waves. All these factors are changed if we allow the folds to weaken and atrophy through underuse and neglect.

The vocal folds weaken and can bow, creating a gap when you try to close them for singing. This gap weakens the resulting sound waves, affecting everything from tone to range and power. When the folds bow due to atrophy and lack of use, they can no longer completely seal when closed, limiting the power they can create. The resulting sound waves will be weak and breathy. You will also lose flexibility, which will impact the range of your voice.

And not to scare you, but if the voice is allowed to atrophy for an extended period, some of what is lost may not be able to be regained. This is why we must strive not to take extended breaks from singing.

So let's protect what we have and build upon it with the 20-5-1- rule!

Now on to our first part of the HEROES System – hydration.

## CHAPTER ELEVEN

# Hydration

Step One of the HEROES SYSTEM

I start with the most obvious but, surprisingly, one of the most neglected aspects of vocal health.

Hydration.

Proper hydration for overall health and efficient voice use is not simply sipping some water when you feel thirsty. Understanding the various aspects of hydration is vital for heavy voice users like singers.

The vocal folds have a purely biological function beyond making sound, acting as a last line of defense to keep food and drink out of our lungs. When something goes "down the wrong way," we start coughing, often quite violently. This cough reflex is the folds pushing the offending material away from the lungs, where it can do damage.

While we are talking about the lungs, the only thing that should ever go into them is…air (and perhaps sterile saline solution; more on that in a bit).

Smoke is particularly detrimental to our physical and singing health, but you know that already.

Water only makes direct contact with your vocal folds if it's gone down the wrong way. Therefore, taking a sip of water to soothe a rough voice due to thick mucus is not as effective as you might think because the water never touches the folds. If it does, you would start coughing to protect your lungs from the liquid.

So, what can we do if what we drink does not reach the vocal folds?

The folds are hydrated in two ways: topical and systemic.

When we are talking about the proper hydration of the folds, we are focusing on the vocal fold mucosa. The folds are comprised of three main layers: ligament, muscle, and outer mucosa. The mucosa is a soft, pliable, mucus-secreting membrane, and it is the most susceptible to injury, the ravages of misuse, and poor vocal hygiene.

It is this outer layer that needs to be hydrated in two ways. The first is systemic hydration, which happens when we drink liquids and eat water-rich foods. The body then allocates the available liquids to the body.

BUT, when it comes to the biological pecking order, the vocal folds are down the list. Singing and communication are wonderful, but your vital organs are more important in the job of staying alive and they get hydrated first.

Consequently, singers need to consume more liquids than the average person. Other factors such as climate, humidity levels, and medications may require you to increase your fluid intake.

Again, it's not just the fluid we drink that affects our hydration levels but also the foods we eat. Water-rich foods like fruits, greens, vegetables, and soups all contribute to our vocal health.

Conversely, overly processed foods do not help hydration and they also affect our energy levels, the gut microbiome, and our health in general. The older we get, the more we should avoid these (admittedly fun) foods.

When we consume liquids, the body sends a certain amount to the surface of the vocal folds. This is the mucus secretion on the outer layer that acts as a lubricant during vocalization. We want this mucus to be thin and plentiful.

Here's where aging creates another challenge. As we age, we deal with decreased saliva and mucus production. Also, the mucus we produce tends to be thicker. This thick mucus is not conducive to singing and can cause us to harshly clear our throats (not good for the vocal folds). Thankfully, increasing hydration levels helps with this.

I also utilize guaifenesin, which is an over-the-counter medication that thins mucus. I take one pill daily, although please consult with your doctor before taking any medications.

Another way to get moisture directly on the folds is environmental. Areas of low humidity are challenging on the voice. Las Vegas performers talk of "Vegas Throat," which is dry vocal folds caused by low humidity levels.

As we breathe in dry air, the air will pass over the vocal folds and dry them out. Breathing through the nose whenever possible is helpful as the air has a better chance of being humidified on its way to the lungs.

If you are in a low-humidity area or your daily humidity will drop in certain seasons, I recommend using a humidifier in your singing area and bedroom. A hygrometer is an inexpensive little device that will tell you the humidity level of your environment. When it drops below 45%, running your humidifier is a good idea.

## Nebulize

Singers often breathe in steam to help with dry folds, but recent research shows that there is a much more effective way to get moisture on your vocal folds and for it to stay there longer. Researchers have found that running a 0.9% saline solution through a mesh nebulizer creates the perfect mist for singers to inhale and coat their folds.

Mesh nebulizers (as opposed to steamers) keep the saline suspended in the mist, and this saline helps the moisture stay on the folds longer. I use a nebulizer throughout the day, and it has a definite positive impact on my voice.

## PTP

Phonation threshold pressure (or PTP) is the measurement of the amount of air pressure needed to get the vocal folds to phonate or make sound. We want this number to be as low as possible because the higher the PTP, the harder the voice has to work. The PTP value changes depending on the pitch and intensity. Higher and/ or louder notes have a naturally higher PTP, which is okay, but we don't want the PTP value higher than necessary.

Dry vocal folds and thick mucus will raise the PTP dramatically. You can experience it for yourself: Lick your lips and buzz them like a trumpet player. Notice how much effort it takes to do this. Now wipe your lips dry and try again. Getting them to vibrate at all likely required more air and pressure at the lips. The entire process is more laborious.

And so it is with the vocal folds. Studies show that the use of a nebulizer with saline solution reduces the PTP in singers.

## Further Issues

Inadequate hydration levels, especially for prolonged periods, negatively affect the folds not just on the surface but also at the cellular level. The physiology of the folds can be affected by prolonged periods of dehydration and can take an extensive period to recover once hydration levels are brought to normal. As we age, we need to do everything we can to keep the tissues and structure of the folds as healthy and pliable as possible.

## Other Liquids

Disclaimer: I am a coffee fanatic. I even buy green beans online and roast them myself. I have complete confirmation bias when it comes to this beautiful beverage.

Having said that, recent research suggests coffee is not the diuretic it was once thought to be, especially for those who have habituated their bodies to regular consumption. However, I suggest supplementing with water when you drink coffee and tea.

If you are not a regular coffee or tea drinker, be careful about consuming them before a performance, as you might experience hydration issues with the voice. Sodas contain water but also a host of chemicals and carbonation, which can exacerbate acid reflux, a terrible condition for singers. The caustic enzyme pepsin (used to digest food) can travel up the esophagus and burn the vocal folds—not something a singer wants.

Reflux can increase with age (and also body weight) so it is helpful to maintain a healthy weight and to avoid spicy foods before bedtime.

There is also a debate about the temperature of the liquids and how it affects the voice. Since the water never touches the vocal folds, the temperature should not have a direct effect, but very cold water can cause muscular constriction around the voice, especially in an already cold environment. As we will see, the voice is a full-body instrument, so constrictions in one part can radiate to other parts of the voice, including the folds.

I drink room-temperature water as a habit. Let your voice be your guide in these matters.

As for how much water to drink, there is no definitive answer because we all have different body sizes and live in different climates with varying diets. Again, the more water-rich your diet is, the less water you need to drink. Drier climates require more fluid intake than humid ones.

That said, the eight glasses a day rule is still a good minimum guide.

In addition, you can monitor the color of your urine to gauge your hydration levels. Clearer is better, or as they say, "pee pale."

You should not allow yourself to get to the point of feeling physically thirsty or getting a dry mouth. Consistent daily hydration is one of your greatest weapons in the fight to keep your voice healthy and agile.

There is no getting around the importance of hydration, so do yourself and your voice a favor. Put down this book, get a tall glass of water, and we will meet again in the next chapter.

## CHAPTER TWELVE

# Exercise

Given everything we've learned, it should come as no surprise that singing is a whole-body sport. The act of singing is irreducibly complex; part of this complexity is the coordination of various parts of the body to create and control our voices in a musical way.

As a voice teacher, I often focus the student on one aspect of the voice to increase awareness and facilitate necessary adjustments. But this "isolating" is an illusion. We cannot separate any part of voice function from the whole. And encompassing this "whole" is the human mind and body.

A handcrafted boutique acoustic guitar can run well over $10,000, and the guitarist who has saved and invested in this instrument is not likely to leave it lying around or exposed to the elements. Rather, this instrument will be cared for, not just because of the money spent, but also out of respect for the quality materials and craft and dedication of the luthier who created it. The instrument is worthy of protection and care because the musician knows and appreciates how special it is.

As the instrument ages, it becomes more precious. Our instrument is far more valuable, unique, and worthy of our care, yet the voice is often taken for granted. We must realize that singing is not just about our vocal folds; it is our entire being. We need to protect and maintain our physical, emotional, and mental health to keep singing at our best levels.

Time will slowly attempt to diminish these gifts, and exercise is one of our best defenses to keep our instrument at peak levels.

## Physical Exercise

There are key areas for singers to focus on: posture, flexibility, balance, endurance, respiratory health, and strength of both core and body. Cardiovascular training such as walking, swimming, and cycling can increase stamina, energy, and lung function, all of which are essential for vocal performance.

Pilates and yoga increase overall strength as well as vital core strength while enhancing flexibility. Breathing exercises are also crucial to keep our lungs, diaphragm, and accompanying muscles of respiration healthy and engaged.

Something as simple as blowing up party balloons is a great way to exercise your breathing mechanism. I use a small device called The Breather Voice that uses inhaling and exhaling resistance to create a fantastic workout.

Choose the type of exercise that works for you and make it a priority. The voice requires the energy and vitality of the whole body to function at its best.

## Vocal Exercise

While this is not a book about how to sing (my book *Beginning Singing* covers this topic in depth), I will give you some basic exercises to help strengthen your instrument.

These are not exhaustive, and if you have current vocal exercises that you like to use, great! What's important are the concepts and reasons behind the exercises.

Again, the battle we are fighting is against weakness, atrophy, and loss of flexibility—all enemies of good singing. Remember, we older singers must work a little harder. Not that we want excess tension (which is never good), but the key word here is "excess."

I tell my students that singing without tension is called "silence." There needs to be tension in the system to set the sound waves in motion and to tune our vocal tract to create helpful, powerful resonances. But I know the word tension is problematic and often associated with strain, so I prefer "toned."

A toned system is one where tensions are appropriately balanced as the body works with and against itself to produce these miraculous vibrations of air. The famous architect Buckminster Fuller created the concept of Tensegrity, where a structure is built not by stacking elements on top of each other but instead held in place by tension. Tensigrity is his combination of "tension" and "integrity."

Simple tensegrity model

Researchers looking into body structure have coined the term "biotensegrity." We are also not elements stacked upon each other but instead held by tension. We need to employ and daily renew this vibrant tension and integrity in our bodies and singing.

As our body starts to weaken, the voice shows the effects. The most common results are loss of range, rough tone, reduced power, and slowing vibrato. In an attempt to correct these issues, the body will turn to the easiest solution: squeezing at the vocal folds.

The squeezing is created by muscles surrounding the folds, and while it can temporarily relieve some conditions such as reduced volume and weak breathy tone, it ultimately creates more issues than it fixes. Squeezing at the vocal folds forces us to use more air to get the folds to phonate (i.e., higher PTP). During the opening and closing cycles, the folds come together with greater force, potentially causing swelling, bruising, and even vocal nodules (small calluses on the surface of the vocal folds).

Instead of putting the load of work on the delicate vocal folds, we can instead direct our energy into anchoring other muscles of the vocal tract and body. Kerrie Obert had me do this as I struggled to deal with my vocal tremor, and I can attest to the powerful results of applying these concepts. I can continue to sing, podcast, teach, and create courses because of these exercises.

In the next chapter, we cover some of these basic yet powerful exercises to keep your voice strong and healthy and to perhaps regain some of what you might have lost.

## CHAPTER THIRTEEN

# Strengthening Exercises

N ote: I have created audio and video supplements for this book and these exercises. Go to maturesinger.com for free access.

I need to start with a disclaimer: If you feel any pain or discomfort from any of these exercises, please stop immediately. Do not push your voice under any circumstances. My advice is to always perform these exercises under the guidance of a qualified teacher.

This is why at <u>VoiceSchool.com</u> we have voice experts available to all members. We even include one-on-one coaching calls as part of the membership so students can ensure they correctly apply these concepts.

For now, I am going to give you the core principles as well as suggested exercises. These guidelines can also be applied to vocal exercises you are doing currently. It's pretty flexible.

## The Breath

What is the best way to breathe for singing? The answer is simple: the one that works best for you. That said, there are certainly sub-optimal ways to breathe and support the voice. The idea of support is to provide the vocal folds with a steady and balanced stream of air that brings the folds into a state of controlled phonation with a minimum of effort.

The old "sing from the diaphragm" maxim is not entirely correct, but it reminds us that the effort should not be at the folds. When we inhale, the diaphragm drops, pulling down on the lungs and creating a vacuum to pull in air. When we exhale, the diaphragm returns to its relaxed condition while the muscles of the ribs and abdomen help expel the air.

We want to keep the muscles strong and the lungs pliable through daily exercise.

One of the best exercises is simply blowing up a party balloon. You will engage both the muscles of inhalation when getting ready to blow air and exhalation as you fill the balloon. The natural resistance of the balloon will work your muscles perfectly.

I also use a hiss to practice proper breathing and resistance. Hold your chest slightly up and open with your ribs expanded, then take a breath and let your tummy expand.

Using a hissing sound, breathe out while keeping your chest and ribs open.

Imagine you are inhaling as you exhale. While not physically possible, this will help create the right dynamic between the opposing muscles of inhalation and exhalation, creating the buoyant feeling of "support."

## The Vocal Folds

Dr. Joseph Stemple is a well-known figure in voice therapy and rehabilitation fields who created the Vocal Function Exercises (VFEs), which have become very popular amongst voice teachers and speech-language pathologists. The exercises are simple yet highly effective. If you are experiencing weakness with your voice, I recommend working VFEs into your daily practice routine.

Starting on C3 (the octave below middle C) for lower voices and C4 (middle C) for higher voice types, hold the O sound (as in the word OLD). Purse your lips like you are sipping through a very narrow straw.

The sound should not be a singing posture; don't try to be loud or brash. It is a soft, steady tone.

Get a timer and see how long you can sustain this pitch. Make a note of the date and length of sustains. You will repeat this process on the notes D, E, F, and G

These exercises help eliminate weak, breathy singing and restore vitality to your voice. Every month or so, revisit how long you can sustain a note. The goal is to go at least twenty seconds. Don't worry if you can't hold the pitch very long; your sustain time will increase with practice.

I have recorded examples of these exercises in the member's area of this book.

## The Vocal Tract

The vocal tract has key components we want to be sure to strengthen. As we discussed in the How The Voice Works chapter, as we change the size and shape of our throat and mouth, we change the resonance of the voice. A readjustment of resonance and vocal tract is necessary for higher notes, particularly when you want to sing with power.

One of the prevalent myths in singing pertains to the concept of the "open throat." This often leads to confusion between the perceived sensation of singing and the actual physiological process involved. For singing with power and stability, especially in higher notes, it's necessary for the throat to narrow, particularly in the upper region.

What we don't want is to squeeze the muscles of the throat around the vocal folds. Phonation without excess squeezing, combined with balanced resonance, feels more "open."

However, we can take this concept too far and open and relax the entire throat, which can also cause issues. The pipe organ is a good visual for this. You can look at the pipes and know which ones are for the lower notes and which are for the higher ones because the length and diameter of the pipes change for each note, with long and wide resonating the low notes and short and thin for high.

Our vocal tract needs to mirror this. If we try to keep our throat too "open" in our upper register, it would be like using a wider pipe for the high note. Therefore, the narrowing and shortening of the vocal tract is essential.

While our "pipe" is much more flexible and complex, the analogy still holds. We need to keep our throat and tongue muscles strong to provide the necessary narrowing and adjustment needed for singing through our entire range.

Kerrie Obert has done over 20,000 endoscopies where she has observed the voice up close through a tiny camera that goes through the patient's mouth or nose. What Kerrie noticed is that all singers, from rock to Broadway to classical sopranos, use narrowing of the upper throat (or oropharynx) when singing higher notes.

Older singers can lose some of this narrowing ability, which creates weaker, less stable high notes. It is essential to work these muscles to regain and maintain this ability.

## The Tongue

The tongue is often misunderstood or neglected in singing, but it should have a leading role, especially for older singers. The tongue is much larger than we realize, with the root of the tongue descending into the upper throat area. The tongue is also unique in the human body. It is not one but numerous muscles that can move independently, like an elephant's trunk.

When the oropharynx narrows, the two lateral sides (left and right) come together towards the middle. However, the throat cannot do this from the front and back without assistance. While the back wall of the throat cannot move, the tongue can do the job from the front.

Moving the back of the tongue (BOT) the back of the throat creates narrowing from front to back. We now have side-to-side (lateral-to-medial) narrowing combined with front-to-back (anterior-to-posterior) narrowing. When coordinated correctly, your voice will be more robust and powerful without straining the vocal folds.

By working the tongue and throat muscles, you will extend the vitality of your voice and find more ease in the high notes. Combine the following strengthening routine with your favorite vocal exercises for maximum benefit.

## Tongue Exercises

Let's work the tongue for strength and coordination. We want to be able to move the tongue forward and backward simultaneously.

Stick out the tip of your tongue and gently hold it between your teeth. Now swallow. You want to accomplish the swallow without the front part of the tongue pulling back.

Let's continue to work the back of the tongue (BOT). Imitate Kermit the Frog or Pee Wee Herman's laugh to the best of your ability. This is accomplished by the BOT pulling back into the upper throat. Sing an EE vowel with your best Kermit voice. Do glides up and down on an interval of a fifth, such as C3 to G3 for low voices and G3 to D4 for higher voices.

Continue to go up by half steps with this exercise, keeping the BOT engaged. Although we will ultimately not sing with quite this exaggeration, this exercise will help build strength and an anchoring for the voice.

Again, we will harness energy and good tension in the vocal tract rather than the vocal folds.

## Twang

We will increase "twang" in the voice for the next exercise. Twang is a term that refers to a brightness facilitated by narrowing the upper throat.

Say NYAH, NYAH, NYAH in a brash, teasing voice. Let it be an exaggeration; it's not a pretty sound. Start at the top of the major scale and walk down an octave with a bratty NYAH on each note. Keep the sound light, small, and UGLY.

I recommend G4 for lower voice and C5 for higher.

As you do this, feel your tongue engage and your soft palate or velum rise. I find it helps to make a squished face as I do this. You can engage muscle as long as you don't squeeze at the folds.

Now take the same approach, but on each note sing YEE, YAY, YAW, YO, YOU. As you do this, press the tongue up and forward and keep everything nasty sounding. Make sure to raise the velum and feel a widening in the back of the mouth.

These are like calisthenics for the vocal tract, so give yourself small breaks as you feel the muscles fatigue.

I have recorded examples of these exercises in the members' area of this book. Go to maturesinger.com to access your free bonus content.

## Effort

As I said before, as an older singer you will need to work harder. A completely relaxed singing technique will fall into the encroaching weakness and atrophy. The stairs we bounded up as a teenager now require more focus and work. The strengthening and working of the vocal tract will give the voice more stability and anchoring and even helps with pitch accuracy.

## Vibrato

One of the tell-tale signs of the older voice is a slower vibrato. A vibrato rate is usually between five and seven cycles per second, also referred to as Hertz (Hz). Whitney Houston was on the slower end at around five Hz and Freddie Mercury was at the faster side at seven Hz. Faster than seven is considered a "tremelo" while slower than five is called a "wobble."

Older voices tend to wobble if the muscles and nerves lose energy and vitality. If I do not energetically engage my vocal tract, a couple of things happen, even on my lower notes.

First, my vocal tremor becomes noticeable, and second, my vibrato moves towards the slower, wobble zone. By anchoring my voice with my vocal tract muscles, my tremor and vibrato are vastly improved.

We'll explore vibrato exercises in a later chapter.

Next, I will introduce you to some of the most powerful exercises singers can do: SOVTs.

## CHAPTER FOURTEEN

# SOVT Exercises

SOVT stands for semi-occluded vocal tract, and research increasingly shows that this should be a regular part of your vocal regimen. SOVT exercises introduce a partial obstruction (semi-occlusion) into the vocal tract, which creates greater pressure and natural resistance in the mouth and throat. The energy of this rising pressure presses down on your vocal folds and helps stabilize them.

By using SOVT exercises, you will experience greater ease and efficiency when phonating or making sound. SOVTs can be accomplished with the lips, tongue, or external devices like straws and kazoos.

Research shows that using a partial obstruction helps eliminate strain or the over-involvement of muscles. The vocal folds need to close against rising air pressure, and the longer the folds stay closed, the more energy is produced in the vocal tract.

Getting a balance between airflow and fold resistance is a large part of the singer's job, and SOVT exercises make this much easier.

Imagine trying to hold down a large helium-filled balloon. Should a powerful fan suddenly appear above and propel a rush of air downwards, the balloon would stabilize and be easier to control

The vocal folds undergo a comparable effect when air pressure is increased from above. (Note: the fancy term is supra-glottal air pressure. Supra means "above" and "glottal" refers to the glottis or opening of the vocal folds.)

Another benefit is that this supra-glottal air pressure creates a "cushion" of air that stops the vocal folds from "slamming together," even when singing with higher intensity levels.

There are several SOVT exercises you can do, from lip trills and voiced consonants to blowing a raspberry while you phonate. There are also specially engineered straws for SOVT exercises that provide the optimal balance of resistance and subglottal pressure.

By running scales, glides, and sustains through bubbling lips or straws, you are, in essence, giving your vocal folds a massage of sorts. Your folds will line up and phonate with increased efficiency and balance while reducing swelling and stiffness.

It's a fantastic warm up!

The research also shows that the balancing benefits from SOVT exercises help the nervous system continue on in the new balance and posture, even after you are done exercising. With repetition, the residual benefits of the SOVT will be there for you during all your vocalizing. Although SOVT exercises are great for every singer, they are especially beneficial for the older voice.

I have created special bonus videos to show you how to do these wonderful exercises. Go to maturesinger.com to access your bonus content.

## Exercises

Straw exercises are the easiest to get started with and provide the most immediate results. Although I have several SOVT devices I recommend in the Resources chapter, we can start off simply. All you need is a drinking straw (preferably one with a flexible bend) and a tall glass half-filled with water.

Place the straw halfway down the water, place your lips like you are getting ready to drink, and "sing" through the straw. You want a steady stream of bubbles, so avoid pushing too much air or the water will fly out of the glass.

Vocalize up and down a scale as the bubbles flow. Move the straw deeper into the water and feel the increased resistance. Move the straw up and down until you find a spot with a nice flow of back pressure into your vocal tract but not so much that you start to struggle or work too hard.

Increase the resistance as you work through these exercises. Longer, thinner straws, and taller, deeper glasses of water increase the back pressure. Play with different levels of resistance.

I also recommend using SOVTs throughout your practice and song work, not just the warming-up phase (although they are great for that). Take a difficult high note and sing it into straw resistance. Feel how it sits in your voice and where the resonance is. Now, sing the note without the straw. You will likely feel an improvement.

You can also do SOVTs without a straw. Voiced consonants such a Z, M, or N will give you an amount of resistance, although not quite as much as a straw. Sticking out your tongue and vocalizing on a "raspberry" is a highly effective SOVT, although you may get some interesting reactions if you do them in public.

SOVTs are an area of voice training that is worth exploring. Play with various resistance levels to see how your voice responds and create custom workouts.

## CHAPTER FIFTEEN

# Range

Over the years, our voices begin to lose elasticity—and there is simply no way around it. For those who were able to reach incredibly high notes in their youth, those extreme notes are likely not coming back.

Menopause, in particular, reduces estrogen levels, often leading to a reduction in the upper range. For singers dealing with menopause, I highly recommend the book, *Singing Through Change* by Cate Frazier-Neely, Joanne Bozeman, and Nancy Bos.

Having gotten the bad news out of the way, we can potentially regain some of our lost high notes even though your voice has experienced changes—and we can certainly slow and delay any further loss of range.

The human body is a wonder we are still striving to understand. One of the more recent discoveries is fascia, which is a band or sheet of connective tissue beneath the skin that attaches, stabilizes, encloses, and separates muscles and other internal organs.

Fascia used to be tossed aside during dissections as a gloppy substance that got in the way of the interesting stuff. The fact is, fascia is one of the most important and fascinating substances in the human body, and its relative health is essential in all movement and, yes, singing.

Fascia is primarily made of collagen and can be hard and stiff one minute and flowing and liquid the next, providing a framework that helps transmit movement and force through the musculoskeletal system. It's like a body suit under our skin that holds us together and assists in movement.

To better understand fascia, I will turn to the children's treat, the gummy worm. My friend and fellow voice teacher Jeremy Ryan Mossman showed me how the gummy worm is a great way to understand the properties of fascia. I now keep a bag of them under my piano so I can show students how it works. Yes, teaching voice is a strange thing without some context.

If you take a gummy worm by both ends and pull it apart sharply, the gummy will stiffen and become somewhat hard. However, the gummy will change if you pull at both ends slowly but steadily. Now, the gummy will begin to thin and lengthen, and the longer you pull it, the more it will stretch.

It turns out the gelatin of gummy worms is made from animal collagen, just like fascia. Vegan gummies do not behave similarly because of the lack of collagen.

Another interesting gummy experiment is to leave one outside of the sealed package. As you would expect, the gummy becomes drier and less flexible over time. This stiffening also happens to your body fascia when it is not properly stretched and exercised.

Thankfully, we can take this dried-out gummy and begin to work and massage it. As we do, the gummy will become more pliable and flexible. When you stretch in the morning, this is not done just for your muscles, joints, and ligaments, but for your fascia that connects it all together.

Keeping the fascia hydrated, flexible, and flowing instead of stiff, dried out, and tight, directly influences your vocal range. When singing a low note, the vocal folds become short and thick. As we ascend in our range, the folds stretch, just like the gummy worm.

If our folds have not been stretched and maintained, they can become stiff and less pliant. The folds can also begin to bow, with the edges no longer aligning correctly. This bowing causes breathiness and a loss of power as the folds cannot come together and seal against the airflow. Again, the body may try and compensate for this by squeezing the folds together, but this inevitably creates more problems than it solves.

If it's been a while since you have worked your full range, fear not! I am here to help you rejuvenate your voice just like the dry, tired-out gummy worm (if you can forgive the comparison).

The best way to drastically reduce the stiffening of your vocal folds is to work your entire range each practice day. Don't focus only on your high notes. Your lower register is equally important, especially for high voice types like sopranos. Don't let this part of your voice become weak with disuse.

Simple glides or phonating through a straw (see SOVT exercises above) from your lowest to highest notes will stretch the muscles, tissues, and ligaments of the vocal folds, but be careful not to push or force the voice. Using a light sound is fine (or even preferable).

If I don't have time for a proper practice session, the one thing I do at a minimum is work my vocal range. A minute or two of gliding up and down my range can help keep my folds and singing mechanism limber and stretched.

If you have lost some of the range that you had in your youth, I want you to embrace your new voice and the excitement you can create. As we age and our voice becomes richer and deeper, we don't need to sing as high to create a thrilling experience for the listener.

Tony Bennett continued to perform into his 90s, even as he battled Alzheimer's disease. While he did not have the same voice he had in the 1950s, it was still a stunning, beautiful, expressive instrument. Tony would still reach an A4—not a note that would make a tenor jealous, but one that in his instrument shot like a beam of light to the listener. Tony continued to rehearse three times a week in his retirement, even as he was often unable to recognize those around him. His joy of singing was unending and infectious.

Please don't mourn over what you think you may have lost. With diligent work, you can recapture some of your range and your mature instrument will bring a new dimension and expressiveness to what you do have. Embrace it!

CHAPTER SIXTEEN

# Range Exercises

The following exercises can help keep your voice stretched and agile. If you have a day with little time for practice, I suggest at least doing some of these as well as SOVT exercises. These simple exercises are not voice builders in the sense we are going to be loud and strong; instead, you can think of them as stretches for the vocal folds that will give you a range (pun intended) of benefits, including enhanced blood flow.

Increased circulation to the vocal folds brings more oxygen and nutrients to the tissue, which is crucial for maintaining vocal fold health. This enhanced blood flow can also accelerate the healing of vocal fold micro-damage that may occur due to extensive use.

These exercises also improve and increase tissue elasticity, which is vital for the proper vibration of the vocal folds during phonation. Regular stretching and exercises that promote circulation can help maintain or improve the elasticity of the vocal fold tissues.

Be on alert for any excess tension during these exercises. One of the hallmarks of our body fascia is its continuous nature. The fascia can spread tension and stiffness from one area to another, so excess tension in your shoulders can work its way into the surrounding muscles of the vocal folds.

As we stretch the muscle and tissue of the folds, the improved circulation and reduced tension can lead to a smoother, clearer, and more consistent voice quality. These are also great exercises when the voice is tired or even a bit hoarse. In this case, keep the exercises on the gentle side and do not continue if there is any pain or discomfort.

## Exercises

Here are some simple exercises to help extend and keep your vocal range: Don't worry if the voice weakens or breaks as you go higher. The one thing we don't want to do is muscle up or squeeze the voice. As you do these exercises daily, the vocal breaks will disappear, especially as you also incorporate the upcoming exercises.

Gliding up and down your range on an OO vowel is a fantastic warmup. Keep the lips extra round and narrow for some SOVT assistance. Then start in your chest voice on a bright AH vowel, and as you glide up, narrow it to OO. Reverse the exercise by starting on a high OO and gliding down to a low AH.

The Y-buzz is a popular exercise that gives a light SOVT effect. Hold out the Y of YES (it is basically an E vowel with a very forward tongue) and purse your lips like you are going to give an air kiss. You should feel a buzz at the front of the mouth and lips. Vocalize through your range on the Y-buzz.

As these exercises feel more comfortable, increase how high and low you go. You will find your range will expand as you warm up (some days may be better than others).

Working both extremes of your range ensures the vocal folds are being stretched properly. By doing these daily, you will feel improvements in your voice.

Now, let's look at optimizing our voice for tone and unity.

CHAPTER SEVENTEEN

# Optimize

Optimizing the voice is a balance of airflow, vocal fold resistance, and resonance. If all three are properly aligned, we can get the maximum range, tone, and power out of our instrument. As we age, this balance becomes crucial to keep our voice healthy, and of the three elements, resonance will make the biggest difference in most voices.

Resonance happens in our vocal tract, the acoustic "tube" of our throat and mouth. Yes, there is some involvement of the nasal passages in certain vocal sounds, but the nose is not a very efficient resonator.

To make sound, we take the flow of air and create disturbances in the air pressure by the closing and opening of the vocal folds. The starts the air molecules moving into patterns of vibration. As noted earlier, these vibrating air molecules need a boost to increase their energy, and our vocal tract does something fascinating with the vibrating air. As we change the size and shape of our vocal tract, we boost some parts of the sound wave and diminish other parts, or partials. This gives us not only different tone colors but also vowels themselves.

But there is something even more profound occurring. As we change the size and shape of the vocal tract, we also help eliminate the vocal break. (This dreaded vocal break is what keeps voice teachers in business.)

The vocal tract contains acoustic resonances, like an acoustic guitar, a violin, or the room you are reading this in. These resonances make certain parts of sound waves louder. Think of clapping in an empty parking garage as opposed to a closet full of clothes.

There are multiple resonances in the vocal tract. The lower resonance boosts lower parts of the sound wave, and the higher resonances boost, you guessed it, higher partials.

When we sing in the lower part of our range (often referred to as chest voice), the lowest resonance does a good deal of the acoustic energizing.

Here is where we run into a problem. As we sing higher, this lower resonance doesn't like to give up the lead role. In order for this lower resonance to attempt to stay up with the rising pitch, it needs to also rise. We accomplish this (or at least attempt to) by contracting our throat and spreading our lips.

The accompanying tension created by this often spreads to the vocal folds. All of this squeezing requires more air pressure to get the folds making sound. The result is basically yelling, which is stressful on the delicate surface of the folds. Not only is this stressful, but it's incredibly inefficient. Ultimately, this first resonance can only go so high, so we now have to let go of everything to keep ascending in pitch.

This creates the yodel or the dreaded vocal break. While a flip or break in the sound can be a useful vocal effect in the right circumstances, it can often cause unintentional vocal disasters.

There is another way to negotiate the higher notes without cracking or strain.

## The Magic of Mix

It goes by many names, but I (and many other voice teachers) call this approach "mix." Mix is a cornerstone of my teaching, and I have even sat on the board of the International Voice Teachers of Mix.

In mix, we still utilize the lower resonance to boost our lower register. But when we ascend in pitch, rather than struggling to keep this low resonance in the dominant position, we back it off and allow the second response to take over more of the workload. When done correctly, this handover allows the singer to move between their lower and upper registers without strain or loss of vocal quality. It sounds like one unified voice.

Even better, this is an optimal way to sing, giving us the most vocal power for the least effort. Most vocal exercises help the singer work on their mix and vocal balance in some way, and while this is not a how-to-sing book (see my book, *Beginning Singing*), I can give you the basic principles of finding your mix.

## Vowels

This idea of controlling our vocal tract resonances is all well and good, but how do we actually do it? With vowels. I am obsessed with vowels. When I toured the UK on a teaching trip, I was bestowed with the moniker, "The Vowel Man," and it's a title I am proud of.

Vowels are the result of specific vocal tract resonances. As we change the size and shape of our resonators and bring out different parts of the sound wave, the main result is different vowels. The acoustics behind it are fascinating, and if you would like to delve deeper, I highly recommend the work of Dr. Ian Howell on Absolute Spectral Tone Color.

Certain vowels are more helpful in making this transition, while other vowels may make it harder. Listen closely to a great vocalist and pay attention to the pronunciation of vowels. You will notice that they change the pronunciation based on how high or low the pitch is, or even the vocal color they wish to achieve.

Vowel modification is a key concept in singing and vocal mix. As you start to get into your vocal transition area, you need to make vowels a bit more narrow or rounded. For example, if you are straining on the word "that," try pronouncing it as "thet." The move from AH to EH will drop the lower resonance and allow the higher resonance to become more involved. In this way, vowel modification can help with vocal optimization.

## Flow

The other aspect of optimizing your voice is the balance of air to vocal fold resistance. We don't want to underpower or overpower our folds with the flow of air, and a concept called "flow phonation" focuses on this balance.

This equation has two elements: the rate of airflow and the amount of fold resistance. The most potentially harmful combination is too much airflow combined with too much resistance, which causes the vocal folds to open and close with excessive energy.

Let's do a quick exercise to demonstrate. Clap your hands at a reasonable volume. You could likely do that for a minute or two. Now, bring your hands together with intensity and force. It doesn't take long for your hands to feel it. Imagine doing this hundreds of times a second, and you get an idea of what your vocal folds go through when they are used this way.

At the other extreme is not enough air or fold resistance, which produces a breathy, weak sound. For most singing, we want balance between airflow and resistance that will give us the best sound waves for our vocal tract to enhance. For softer singing, this would be less flow and resistance, and for more robust singing, it would be greater flow and resistance, without pushing to the unhealthy extremes. A big part of breath control is keeping this air flow rate optimal for the pitch and intensity level you desire.

Whatever your vocal practice routine, be sure to focus on balancing your airflow, fold resistance, and vocal resonance.

## Registration

The voice is an instrument of registers, and vocal registers are a subject of much debate amongst voice teachers. I will give you my viewpoint on the matter.

The two primary registers of the voice are commonly called "chest" and "head." The chest register encompasses our lower range and is so named because the sensations of resonance are felt vibrating the sternum or chest. The head register is our higher notes, and more of the sympathetic vibrations and sensations of the sound waves are felt in the head.

There are other names for these, such as mode one (M1) and mode two (M2). I still use head and chest as they are terms of sensation, and much of what we experience is sensation-based.

The key area for optimization and balancing is the area between the two registers as we shift from chest to head or vice versa. The voice will undergo shifts, both physical and acoustic. The folds will go from short and thick to long and thin as we ascend, and the acoustics will change their relationship to the sound waves. We want to make this transition as smooth as possible.

In the next chapter, we will explore exercises (and the concepts behind them) to optimize and registrate the voice.

## CHAPTER EIGHTEEN

# Optimize Exercises

These exercises will build upon the range work we have been doing so far. With these exercises, we want to aim for tone, resonance, and registration. These will also help you find your mix or smooth blending between the chest and head voice. These exercises will help you sing high notes with less effort (although not a complete absence of effort) and will also eliminate vocal breaks or cracking.

Take your time, and be patient; your efforts will be well rewarded. The work of optimizing and balancing the voice is never done, and it is a daily job for singers to keep these coordinations finely tuned.

## Controlling Resonance

Resonance is a singer's best friend and the solution for many vocal issues. This is why learning to control the vocal tract resonances is one of the top skills I focus on with clients.

Changes in our instrument can play with the delicate coordinations, sensations, and perceptions of these resonances, so we are constantly rebalancing the voice from year to year (even day to day). Since we cannot see these resonances, we must guide them by the resulting sensations. Mind-body awareness is essential for this.

You can apply these concepts to the vocal exercises of your choice. I will give you a couple of my favorites here.

## Exercises

Make an NG sound as in the word SUNG, then hold this sound and glide up and down. Pay careful attention to where you feel the vibrations of the voice, especially as you move up and down.

While individual experiences can vary, most singers feel the vibrations of the voice move above the soft palate or velum to somewhere behind the eyes. This sensation of shifting resonance becomes the pathway for eliminating vocal breaks and balancing vocal registers.

Next, using the word WON, take a scale from your lower to upper register and be careful not to allow the vowel to open up toward AW or AH. The UH of WON is a great vowel for keeping the resonances balanced as we sing higher.

Another favorite of mine is BOOH, as in BOOK. BOOH also keeps the resonances balanced, and the back pressure of the B consonant helps to stop the larynx or voice box from rising and squeezing.

You can explore vowel tuning and vowel adjustments to help move from chest voice to head voice. Take a scale and start with the word WAY. As you sing higher, change the word to WEE. You should feel a greater ease and a smoothing of the break when doing this.

Once these exercises are working for you, apply the concepts from the Strengthening Exercises chapter. Activate the tongue (especially the back of the tongue) and vocal tract to help anchor you as you sing. Be sure to lift the velum and feel the back of your oral cavity widen.

Continue to extend your range and intensity with your chosen scales.

If you would like some examples of exercises, please go to maturesinger.com to access the bonus section for this book.

## Vowel Tuning

Vowels are the secret key to balanced, efficient singing. By adjusting and tuning the vowels, we are changing the size and shape of our vocal tract. When done correctly, these changes create optimal relationships between the sound waves and the vocal tract resonances.

Here is a quick chart to help you get started on this concept.

BAT-BET-BIT-BEET
BOT-BUT-BOOK-BOOT

If you are struggling with singing a word, find the vowel sound on the chart above.

In "Rolling in the Deep," Adele hits a climactic note on the word "all." This part of the song is difficult for many singers because of the pitch, intensity, and the vowel. The AH sound of "all" is an open vowel, which lends itself to yelling and straining.

Using the above chart, the vowel sound of "all" is the same as BOT, but if we move one vowel to the right, we replace the AH sound of BOT with the UH of BUT.

In the case of "Rolling in the Deep," replacing "AHL" with "UHL" will adjust the vocal tract to let go of the yell tuning and allow the resonance to align better with the sound waves.

Use the chart above on a song you struggle with and see if it helps. While singers of all ages can be helped by utilizing vowel adjustments, older singers in particular need to watch for heaviness and strain. Again, the vocal folds can thicken and become less pliable as we age, so these imbalances in registration can be magnified. Vowel tuning is one of the best ways to help balance and registrate the voice.

CHAPTER NINETEEN

# Energy

*"No one is as old as those who have outlived enthusiasm."*
– Henry David Thoreau

E
nergy is essential in singing and performance, and older singers need to harvest and utilize energy more intensely than our younger selves. Here I use the word "energy" in a holistic sense, and we want our singing to be energized in the voice and the entire body and mind.

This "work" is not excess tension or strain, but rather a fight against the realities of the aging process—atrophy, muscle weakness, reduced lung capacity, and the stiffening of muscles, ligaments, and body fascia.

Energy and mental focus are some of our greatest weapons against the creeping of time. Remember, we are model of biotensegrity (biology + tension + integrity), and our energy will support this healthy tension to create integrity and stability in our singing and very being.

# Imagery

As we have seen throughout these chapters, working the mind is as important as working the physical voice, and we need to develop strong mental connections to our instrument. Imagery is a wonderful way to control the incredibly complex act of singing. By finding vocal balance and then attaching powerful imagery, you will be better able to reconnect to these coordinations quickly.

When I feel myself slouching, rather than thinking about standing straighter, I create imagery of my head floating like a balloon. If I am giving a public talk or singing masterclass, I will imagine my energy filling the room. When I need to sing a high note, I don't allow myself to reach up but instead take the position of being above the note and placing it below me.

The great thing about imagery is you can experiment with it and create images and mind pictures that work for you. By all means, do not try to force someone else's imagery on yourself if you find it does not work.

When I first started teaching, I was warned against using imagery as a type of "vocal voodoo." I believe this caution was well-meaning but ultimately wrong. The bad reputation of imagery was partly because students would try to force the imagery their teacher gave them. But imagery only works if it truly makes sense to you.

I also encourage singers to learn as much as they can about the anatomy and acoustics of the voice because the more precise you are with body mapping, the better you can form effective imagery.

## Vibrato

One of the telltale signs of an aging voice is a slower, wider vibrato. By employing more energy and activating muscle tone in the vocal tract (rather than gross tension), the vibrato can be sped up and the voice will appear more youthful and livelier. Energy in our posture, breath, vocal tract, tongue, and even in our emotional intentions will all come together to give longevity and vibrancy to your voice.

As we've discussed, there needs to be good appropriate tension in the body and instrument. I prefer to call this good tension "tone." Training the older voice requires moving energy away from the vocal folds and into the vocal tract, velum, and tongue.

This is not excessive tension but energetic muscle tone, and vibrato in particular responds to this greater body energy and good tension. I often refer to vibrato as the canary in the vocal coal mine. Your vibrato will tell you if the voice is out of balance or lagging.

## Body Work

Engaging the whole body helps support your singing in new and vibrant ways. We will look at some exercises to help you create and release more energy while keeping the body limber and agile, avoiding over-tensing and straining.

## Emotion

Emotional energy is a big part of why people listen to singers. I tell my students the highest level of singing is not technique but communication and connection. By infusing our singing with honest emotion, we can experience new levels of communication, vibrancy, and an energetic renewal.

Energy feeds emotion, and emotion feeds energy. We will look at how to find and sustain emotional connection in every moment of a song.

## Be Here Now

By clearing the mind, we open ourselves to the nuances of the voice and musicality. I find mindfulness exercises to be essential to fight through the "fog of war" that we can sometimes experience in performance and even practice. Being open to the full body experience—as well as to the micro-changes that singing can bring—allows us to make better decisions and adjustments.

## Learning an Instrument

Music is a fantastic way to keep the brain active and preserve our ability to learn. Puzzles and chess can also be beneficial, but I find music to be the greatest puzzle of all.

I suggest learning a musical instrument to further enhance learning and cognitive function.

The ukulele in particular is a wonderful, inexpensive instrument that is also relatively easy to play. I am such a believer in this that I include piano and ukulele courses in my VoiceSchool.com.

If you already play an instrument, fantastic! Keep this as part of your daily musical life.

CHAPTER TWENTY

# Vibrato Exercises

Vibrato is essentially a body tremor. While researchers are still figuring out the how and what of vibrato, there are approaches to help get into the energetic zone of five-to-seven cycles per second. We will expand on some of the concepts from the Exercise chapter as well as imagery and body movement.

When I sing, I connect my vibrato to my emotional and physical energy. You can practice this by getting into an emotional state of nervousness or the feeling of being on the edge of crying. Say the phrase "Oh no!" while feeling your body begin to slightly shake. Let the nervous emotion into your voice, allowing it to tremble and shake slightly. We are not singing yet, just getting the body and nervous system ready.

Next, hold your hands in front of you and tremble them. Feel the speed and sensations of this trembling. You will notice that your brain is not actively involved in the back-and-forth motions of the tremble. Once it is set in motion, it is somewhat self-sustaining. As your hands tremble, sustain YEE on a comfortable note.

Allow the tremble of the hands to activate your vibrato. Don't force it, allow to happen like your hands–it's self-sustaining.

Next, let's work sustains with and without vibrato. By employing energy and muscle tone in the voice, we can work on keeping our sustains and vibrato vibrant and spinning.

Find a comfortable note in your lower register and sustain an EE vowel. Take note of the resulting tone and vibrato (if any). Now, lift the velum, widen the back of the mouth, and move the tongue back toward a slight "Kermit the Frog" sound.

Hold the pitch on a straight tone (without vibrato) and then allow the vibrato to come in without losing the muscular engagement of the vocal tract. Don't force the vibrato but rather let it be like the tremble. Use your hands if it helps. You should experience the vibrato speeding up with less variation in pitch. Go back and forth between straight tone and vibrato.

Next, go to a song that is not too difficult but has a number of sustains ("The Rose" by Bette Midler works well for this). Before you begin, create a heightened emotional state of nervousness or sadness and feel the body slightly tremble. When you come to the sustains, hold your hands out and tremble them, feeling this energy move through your body to your voice. Allow a subtle vibrato (not forced) into your sustains. You should feel the combination of energy and emotion come together to speed up your vibrato.

A proper vibrato will give your voice a new vitality and youthful perception, but this can take time, so be patient with yourself. I have recorded examples of these exercises in the members' area of this book. Go to maturesinger.com to access your bonus content.

## CHAPTER TWENTY-ONE

# Body Work

O ur muscles, body, and sense of energy should be in a state of readiness whenever we sing. By focusing on and engaging all of our energy, the muscles receive impulses from the brain and are poised to engage in balanced contraction. Our expansion of energy is also helpful for dynamic, engaging performances.

Before I engage in singing (either performing or practice), I will focus on all corners of the space I am currently in. I will then mentally place a shining star in each corner and concentrate on sending my awareness and energy to them. I fill the space with my mental, physical, and soon-to-be acoustic presence. By engaging in this way, I am more dynamic and my body is ready for work.

By being very present, I am readying the muscles for work by firing low levels of stimulus to them. As this stimulus increases, the excitation threshold will be passed and contractions will begin. By maintaining heightened energy and awareness, I am better able to control the degrees of contraction finely, enabling focused and energized vocalizing without excessive muscular tension.

Excessive tension is something we should always be on guard against. Because of the nature of our body fascia, tension and movement in one area will radiate through the body. The recommended exercises to help increase body energy include pilates, yoga, or movement disciplines like the Alexander or Feldenkrais techniques.

## Movement for Singing

Singing is a high-level skill, and it is easy to become overly rigid while trying to control our instrument. Thankfully, there are a number of movements that can be helpful for singers. Your arms, in particular, are fantastic for helping free up the ribcage and back and neck muscles.

Try lifting your hands up to the ceiling and feeling your torso lengthen and ribcage expand. Take in a deep relaxed breath and vocalize a scale of part of a song. Did you feel the voice open up?

Now, slowly drop your arms while maintaining this feeling of lengthening and expansion. Rolling your shoulders and swinging your hips Hula-Hoop-style can also keep the body activated yet flowing.

As you practice, let your hands guide your voice. Let them reach forward as you sustain, or shake your hands during vibrato. The visual and kinesthetic feedback from these movements helps us connect deeper with actions in the voice.

Our bodies are continuous and everything affects everything, especially the fascia that is so important in movement.

CHAPTER TWENTY-TWO

# Emotional Expression

*"It's like you trade the virility of the body*
*for the agility of the spirit."*
– Elizabeth Lesser

E motional expression is a crucial aspect for singers, especially as we age. What we might lose in range or power can be replaced with our deep emotional well of experience. We have all heard technically astounding singers who leave us a little cold and unmoved with their singing. And then there are those whose voices are less than perfect but leave us in pure joy or a puddle of tears.

Such is the power of emotion. And of the two extremes, I will choose emotional communication and connection over technical perfection.

Part of my work as a voice teacher is to help public speakers and executives powerfully deliver their message. One of the key components I teach is emotional intentions. I learned this from a top Hollywood acting teacher, Carole D'Andrea. Her class is so popular that on my first day, I was seated next to an Oscar-winning actress who was also there to learn.

Talk about intimidation!

But to my surprise, Carole's methods were simple and powerful. By utilizing intentions rather than blanket emotions, I was able to capture deeper parts of my core being in song.

The energy of real, pulsating human emotion cannot be denied. It infuses the singer and listener with a beautiful, ancient connection of humanness. I have heard a singer's technique improve from being guided into a real emotional connection with the song.

## Emotional Intentions

My initial attempts at performance in Carole's class were less than stellar. At first I tried to force somewhat benign emotional stances like "sad" or "angry" into my singing, but I learned from Carole that rather than forcing a nebulous or vague emotional concept, the best approach was to utilize the power of intention.

I delve into this subject in my book *The Compelling Speaker,* as intentions are not just for acting and singing. I have adapted some of the concepts from that book here.

Actors use techniques known as objectives and intentions to achieve emotional authenticity. In every interaction, we have a desire, whether broad or specific. If your overarching aim in a song is to break up a relationship, that's your objective, your primary desire.

To accomplish this objective, you employ various intentions. Intentions are dynamic verbs that define your immediate desires in a conversation, and they can shift as the interaction evolves, even if the overall objective stays constant.

We're constantly using intentions, often subconsciously, and they hold immense power and can imbue your voice with conviction and authenticity. A common error singers make is trying to force a specific emotion (e.g., "I'm going to be enthusiastic"), but this often comes across as insincere.

Instead of focusing on feeling "sad" or "angry" in a song, the vocalist might choose intentions like "to confront," "to reject," or "to implore." These choices reflect what the singer wants in that moment and naturally generate emotion.

Instead of forcing an emotion in your song, you can establish a sequence of intentions. For example, if we have a lyric like "and so this is goodbye," what intentions can be used? Ask yourself, why is this being said? It's not simply to say "goodbye." Intentions could include "to rebuke," "to shame," "to comfort," or "to mourn."

Imagine yourself singing this line with different intentions. See how much changes? Depending on your focus and commitment level, each intention will activate different emotional responses in the body and nervous system. These varying emotions will almost effortlessly transfer to the voice, influencing your tone, volume, timing, and phrasing.

Intentions also create differing body language, eye contact, posture, countenance, and emotional energy. We all know the impact of a genuinely charismatic individual entering the stage. But what is charisma? It's not about forced smiles or feigned emotion. Authentic charisma radiates from someone who fills the space with sincere, heartfelt energy and passion, not something fabricated.

If your sole intention in that moment is to truly comfort, or rebuke, the audience will perceive and respond to it. Your voice will convey this genuine emotional intent as you sing, naturally resulting in charisma. The clearer and stronger your intention, the more palpably it will resonate throughout the room.

The universe operates on vibrations; your voice is vibration, and so is emotional energy. These vibrations resonate with the listener's brain, creating a harmonious frequency. Your emotionally charged, melodious voice will "vibrate" with your listeners.

As you express your true emotional self, you'll feel the audience's energy reverberating back to you, culminating in genuine confidence. It's a magnificent cycle of energy exchange with emotional intentions at its heart.

## Increased Energy

Another benefit of genuine emotional connection and expression is the energy it creates within us. When employing intentions, the resulting emotions energize our voice and body.

I remember watching singers struggle in Carole's class, and my inner voice teacher thought of the technical adjustments that could be made. Carole, however, did a few simple exercises to connect them emotionally with the song.

And to my surprise, not only did they sing with more emotion, but many of their technical issues disappeared as well. Such is the power of emotional energy.

## CHAPTER TWENTY-THREE

# Mindfulness and Meditation

started meditating a few years ago, and it has had a profound effect on my mental health and well-being. My ability to reset and refocus has been greatly enhanced, as has my ability to stay focused when practicing or even writing this book.

Meditation does not have to be on a pillow with incense burning. You can meditate while walking, doing the dishes, or singing. It is the practice of catching and stopping yourself from being identified with thought and then allowing yourself to be pure experience. Only seeing, only hearing, only being.

Applying this selfless experience to singing helps remove performance anxiety and critical self-talk. Your performing and practicing will be enhanced when you can effortlessly access the "flow state" where you are so consumed in the doing that you lose track of self and time. It's beautiful!

## Getting Started

I recommend using guided meditations. There are several apps you can use, but my personal favorite is the Waking Up app.

Most meditations start with focusing on the breath. You could meditate focusing on your thumbs, but the breath is an ever-flowing passive action, so it is a good place to start.

Everyone struggles to maintain their focus, especially at first. The meditator starts focusing on the breath, but random thoughts soon pull them away. A beginner will often view this as a failure as they struggle to refocus on their breathing, only to have their mind wander again.

But catching yourself in thought and refocusing on your breath IS the "practice" of meditation. It's analogous to lifting weights at the gym. Each time you catch yourself lost in thought, it's another "rep" that strengthens your meditation and focusing skills.

The ability to focus without judgment or distraction will serve you well in singing. While the scientific findings on meditation are mixed, there does seem to be evidence of improvement in the areas of stress, anxiety, and depression.

I personally find meditation has additional benefits for the singer.

## In the Practice Room

When I practice, I remove all distractions from my environment. At certain times during my practice, I allow myself to go into a state of non-dual awareness. Rather than thinking about me and my breathing or me and my vocal folds, I allow pure experience with no judgment.

A good question to ask yourself is, "What if there were no problem to solve?" This query leads me to let go of self-criticism and the need to control. A purely sensory experience often follows. It's no longer me and my voice, but only the voice. There is only vibration, there is only sound, there is only energy.

While these experiences can be brief, they often give me a new insight into the act and experience of singing.

Keep a journal in your practice area and take notes of your thoughts and insights. Review these notes when you are not practicing and see what guidance is there for you.

## Body Energy

I will also meditate to experience my body energy. I first feel myself sitting, and then I allow my focus to perceive the body as a cloud of tingling and vibrating sensation. I then imagine my body shooting light and filling the room. This is one way to tap into your natural, vibrating energy. And finally, I begin singing, allowing the energy to permeate my space.

## The Illusion of the Self

The following meditation can seem a bit "out there," but it has been extremely helpful for me. There are forms of meditation that point to the sense of self as an illusion. This understanding comes from observing thoughts, feelings, and sensations as fleeting phenomena rather than as defining aspects of one's identity. For singers, this perspective can be transformative.

By employing this non-dual awareness, you eliminate the subject-object perspective we commonly employ, and move into a sense of just being. This helps facilitate the flow state, a hallmark of great athletes and performers.

In flow, energy is not directed inward and is devoid of self-talk, especially criticism. It is replaced by pure experience, where we become one with everything around us. Our ability to hear the music and allow our honest emotions to fill the core of our singing is a sublime experience, and the energy generated by this mindset is extraordinary.

One simple way to direct yourself to this perspective is to look at something, such as an object on your desk or the wall. This creates the subject-object experience of me, here, looking at that, over there.

Now, turn your focus inward and look for what's looking. Can you find yourself?

It turns out, when looking for the "self" there's nothing to find, at least not in the way we typically think of the self residing behind our eyes. What I experience is the object I am looking at is no longer over there. It's all pure experience. These insights are brief, but they can open your awareness to new energy, connection, and levels of performance.

I recently worked with a talented musical theatre performer who came to me to help find her strong belt voice. Once we balanced the air, folds, and resonance, I had her raise her arms, shake her hands, and feel the vibrancy of her emotional core.

"Now sing!"

Her voice was suddenly massive and wonderfully passionate.

I asked her what it felt like, and her answer was a perfect illustration of this chapter.

"I disappeared."

Her singing was so wonderfully connected to her emotion and energy that she was in pure experience. This is the magic of mindfulness and energy.

CHAPTER TWENTY-FOUR

# SING!

The final step in the HEROES System is the most important—we need to sing! And I mean sing every day and everywhere you can.

The lift in your physical and emotional well-being will be profound, as singing is one of the best ways to stay healthy, positive, and socially active. Especially for aging singers, I recommend incorporating singing into your daily life. Find moments throughout your day, whether during a shower, cooking, or a solitary walk in nature, to let your voice ring out. This sharpens your skills and integrates singing into your daily routine.

Select songs that hold personal significance and resonate with you. A deep connection to the music elevates the joy of singing and intensifies your emotional bond. Work on different intentions and allow the song to take on new emotional dimensions.

And don't be afraid to shake things up. Find new genres and styles. Listen to new artists and absorb their artistry, allowing it to bring a variety of options to your voice.

## Go Live

Singing for and with others is the highest level of the singing experience. Nothing will increase your abilities, connection, and enjoyment quite like performance.

I recommend that you engage with a community, like a choir or local theatre group. Such involvement goes beyond singing; it's about being part of a group that shares your enthusiasm. These communities of like-minded individuals offer a supportive atmosphere for vocal and emotional growth.

Open mic nights or even karaoke are also great ways to share your gifts with others. The opportunities to sing and grow in your knowledge of this art form are endless.

## Record

Another way to grow in this art form is to record yourself. It doesn't have to be in a formal recording studio (although that is also an intense and beneficial learning experience). A laptop, some software, and a $100 USB microphone are all you need to get started. You can use pre-existing karaoke tracks at first and start laying down your vocals.

Home recording is a great hobby that will put your singing under the microscope, allowing you to perfect your vocal performances.

## Regular Study

I encourage you to expand your knowledge about all things singing consistently. Reading technical books and artist biographies is a wonderful way to grow your knowledge and passion. Just one new insight or bit of knowledge makes a book worthwhile.

Taking formal lessons is one of the best things you can do for your voice. It keeps you accountable, and the right teacher can guide you with exercises appropriate for your current level. Online courses can also be a fantastic way to learn, and they are even better if there is an accompanying live coaching element.

There are more resources to learn and perform than ever before. Focus on what interests you and see where it leads.

CHAPTER TWENTY-FIVE

# Health Benefits

have referenced the physical and mental health benefits of singing throughout the book, but I wanted to bring it together with a deeper focus here. Consider this my final sales pitch to keep you singing!

The physical benefits of singing are wide and varied. You will experience improved repository function, as regular singing and practicing will increase your lung capacity and strengthen the muscles of respiration.

Singing is also an aerobic exercise, especially when done with energy and vitality. Singing and performing will increase your heart rate and will be helpful with overall cardiovascular health. You will also improve your posture and build vital muscle and strength in your core, assisting in balance and spinal health. Your speaking voice and communication will improve with better tone, strength, and clarity.

Your immune system also benefits. While listening to music can help reduce stress hormones, the act of singing also increases antibodies that help fight off infections. Regular singing also releases endorphins, which can act as a natural pain reliever.

So many physical downsides of aging can find relief in consistent singing practice.

## Cognitive Benefits

The body is not the sole recipient of singing's gifts. There are a host of neurological and cognitive benefits as well. Singing activates various parts of the brain to support neural health and potentially delay cognitive decline. It also involves coordination of different motor skills, which helps maintain motor function.

The act of singing involves complex cognitive processes since learning lyrics and melodies stimulates memory and recall. Neuroscientific studies have shown that engaging in musical activities can enhance neural plasticity, which means a sharpened memory and a more agile mind to fend off age-related decline.

Neuroplasticity, or brain plasticity, refers to the brain's ability to change and adapt as a result of experience. This adaptability includes the brain's capacity to reorganize itself by forming new neural connections throughout life, which is crucial for learning new skills and adapting to new situations or environmental changes.

Contrary to earlier beliefs, it's now understood that the human brain retains a significant degree of plasticity throughout life, including in older age. This means that the brains of older adults can still create new neural pathways and adapt to new learning and experiences.

Continued learning and cognitive engagement are crucial for maintaining neuroplasticity. Activities that challenge the brain, like learning a new language, playing a musical instrument, or (no surprise) singing can help keep the brain agile.

Since singing requires concentration, it can improve attention span and mental clarity. It's akin to a workout for the brain, keeping it active and engaged.

## Emotional Well Being

Singing makes you happier. It feeds the brain and your emotional reward centers. Singing also helps keep you active and social, which are key for mental health and well-being. Singing, especially in choirs or groups, fosters a sense of community and belonging. It's not just about the music but the connections formed and the shared joy of creation.

Learning and improving on a high-level skill like singing can significantly boost self-esteem and confidence. Some studies suggest that engaging in creative and social activities like music and singing may contribute to a longer life expectancy. This is likely due to the combined physical and mental health benefits and the positive impact of social engagement. Singing is life-changing and life-affirming, and it is one of the most powerful activities we can undertake as we age.

Utilizing the HEROES System and committing to the 5-20-1 rule will keep your voice vital and healthy and allow it to pay you back in beautiful ways.

Singing is truly a lifelong gift you give yourself.

CHAPTER TWENTY-SIX

# Voice Doctors

An Ear, Nose, and Throat doctor (ENT) is invaluable for the singer, especially as we age. ENTs who focus on the voice (and receive additional training) are called laryngologists and are often preferred.

You will likely be "scoped" with a laryngoscope device when visiting an ENT. This device contains a camera that records a video of your throat and vocal folds (more on this in a bit).

The scope has two main varieties: flexible and rigid. The flexible scope is more common and is inserted through the nose and down into the pharynx or throat. A topical anesthetic is applied to the nasal cavity to make this less daunting for the patient. It sounds worse than it is (at least in experience!).

The rigid scope is a long metal wand that enters through the mouth. The rigid scope tends to have better resolution and can help the doctor with a trickier diagnosis.

Stroboscopy adds a microphone and a strobe light to the scope. The microphone estimates the voice's pitch and the vocal fold vibration rate. The strobe will then time its flashing to the pitch to capture a "slow motion" version of the vocal folds in action, allowing the doctor to view the folds as they phonate. Note: the vocal folds vibrate too quickly for the naked eye to view without this strobe effect.

Take your phone camera and record a video when the doctor plays back the results for you. It's fascinating, and you can send the video to other voice experts for additional opinions.

## Seeking Treatment

You should seek out an ENT when you experience persistent changes in the voice lasting more than two weeks. These changes and issues can include hoarseness, raspiness, or a significant reduction in range

It's also important to pay attention if you're experiencing difficulty or discomfort while swallowing. Any continuous pain in your throat should be looked at by a medical professional.

Breathing difficulties, including shortness of breath, wheezing, or other challenges related to vocal activity are equally concerning. If you find your voice getting tired easily, or if you're losing vocal endurance in ways that aren't typical for you, it's a sign to seek advice. If you find yourself frequently needing to clear your throat or if you have a persistent cough, especially in relation to singing, this could be a warning sign.

Be attentive to any noticeable lumps, bumps, or swelling in the neck or throat area. Changes in your overall health, such as following a respiratory infection, surgery, or starting new medications that seem to affect your voice should not be overlooked.

Even if you aren't experiencing any symptoms, periodic check-ups are beneficial, particularly for professional voice users. An ENT specialist can offer tailored advice, diagnosis, and treatment plans. They can also guide you on vocal hygiene and preventive measures to keep your voice in its best condition.

## Medications

When being prescribed new medications, check to see if any of the side effects can cause singing issues, especially medications that cause drying. Remember, fully hydrated vocal folds are much easier to sing with. Ask your pharmacist or check out the full guide at the National Center for Voice and Speech. ncvs.org/prescriptions

## CHAPTER TWENTY-SEVEN

# Real Life Experiences

*"It gets better as you get older. Don't be afraid, be smart."*
– Advice to a younger singer.

In preparation for this book, I surveyed a group of singers over fifty. I asked questions ranging from their difficulties, how their habits have changed, and what advice they would give younger singers. The answers were in some ways predictable, but also fascinating and inspiring.

Older singers are playing in punk bands, and bringing down the house at karaoke clubs by belting out AC/DC. They are performing with younger musicians and beatboxers, and exploring new styles of music.

They are also singing in church and for friends and family. These singers have found (which mirrors my experience) that singing and music become more precious and important as we age. Many singers are having the best musical times of their lives, even while navigating the challenges of the older voice.

The singers all emphasize health, practice, and continuous learning as cornerstones of their singing lives, and strongly urge younger singers to adopt the same focus and discipline early to keep their voice functioning at its best.

## Accepting Change

Many of these vocalists have lost some of their highest notes but find new musical expression in the depth and richness of their current voices. As one singer reported, "It's not just about hitting the right notes anymore; it's about understanding and respecting my voice's new boundaries."

Another singer remarked, "I've started focusing more on songs that celebrate the warmth and depth of my current range rather than lamenting the notes I can no longer reach."

This shift in repertoire is a common theme, reflecting a deeper appreciation and understanding of their matured voices.

## Emotional Journey

The emotional journey of singing post-50 is filled with depth and introspection. As the physical aspects of the voice change, so does the emotional connection to singing.

"There's a story in every note I sing now, a reflection of my life's journey," reflected one singer. Emotion is a powerful tool, allowing singers to connect with their audience on a deeper level.

Many respondents spoke of a newfound freedom in expression, unburdened by the expectations of youth. One said, "I sing with more honesty and emotion now. My voice carries the experiences of my life, and that's something you can't replicate."

Over decades, the accumulated experience of singing becomes a profound asset for older artists. This experience transcends technical skill, encompassing an emotional and interpretative depth that enriches their performances.

"There's a certain confidence and authenticity that comes with age," one singer told me. "I understand the stories behind the songs more deeply and convey them with a sincerity that only comes from having lived those emotions."

## Physical and Mental Wellness

Maintaining physical and mental wellness plays a significant role in supporting vocal health at this stage. The survey responses highlighted a strong connection between overall well-being and vocal performance.

"Yoga and meditation have become as integral to my singing as vocal warm-ups," one singer reported, which highlights the importance of holistic health practices.

Mental wellness, too, is a key factor. The stress of adapting to a changing voice can be significant, and many singers over 50 emphasize the need for mental resilience.

One singer shared, "Staying positive and mentally agile helps me navigate the challenges with more grace and less frustration."

The narratives of singers over 50 are as diverse as they are inspiring. They navigate the physical and emotional changes of their voices with resilience, adapting their techniques and embracing the unique qualities that age brings to their art.

Their journey is a testament to the enduring power of music and the human spirit. In understanding their experiences, we gain insight into the complexities of vocal evolution and the broader lesson of embracing change and finding beauty in every stage of life.

Through their stories, these artists remind us that the journey of music, much like life, is ever-evolving and filled with continuous learning and profound joy. As one singer summed it up, "My last breath will probably be a nice tune."

CHAPTER TWENTY-EIGHT

# Next Steps

*"I am of the opinion that my life belongs to the whole community, and as long as I live, it is my privilege to do for it what I can."*
– George Bernard Shaw

## An Invitation

My full-time focus is helping others sing and keep the joy of music in their lives. I have spent the last two years building what I believe is an unprecedented singing resource that bridges the gap between private lessons, online study, community, and performance.

VoiceSchool.com has a growing library of cutting-edge courses, including resources for the older singer. It also has a wonderful online community where you can get answers from me and the voice experts on my team, as well as supportive feedback for your singing.

In addition, members receive an initial live vocal diagnostic with a voice expert so they know what to work on, and we continue the personal support with our one-on-one vocal check-ins. Anytime you feel stuck, you can get on a call with one of my voice experts and they will assist you.

You always have an actual human there to assist you personally.

If this resonates with you (both in your voice and being), I invite you to join me and my voice professionals in VoiceSchool.com.

You can get a free 14-day trial by going to voiceschool.com/free

I look forward to working with you and your voice.

Yours in proudly growing older,
John

## CHAPTER TWENTY-NINE

# Resources

The following is a list of resources to help you on your life-long singing journey.

## SOVT Tools

Semi-occluded vocal tract exercises are key for keeping the voice balanced and in shape. Specialized straws and tools are now developed for singers and professional voice users. I use all of the following and highly recommend them:

The Voice Straw: This set of highly versatile straws was designed by celebrity voice teacher Mindy Pack in collaboration with SOVT pioneer Dr. Ingo Titze. I recommend getting the accompanying cup set, which allows you to articulate and sing words while doing SOVT exercises. voicestraw.com

Doctor Vox: A highly effective portable water and straw kit endorsed by well-known voice coach Jaime Vendera. doctorvox.com

Vocal Tubes: UK vocal coach Joshua Alamo has created these large flexible tubes to be utilized with bottles of water. vocaltubes.com

Oovo Straw: The Oovo Straw necklace is a wonderful and functional piece of jewelry. Have an SOVT straw handy at all times! oovostraw.com

I also have a free course on warming up with straws available here: strawarmups.com

Breather Voice: This portable device creates adjustable resistance on inhales and exhales. A few minutes a day will keep your respiratory muscles strong and vibrant. pnmedical.com

## Information Resources:

Kerrie Obert is a pioneer in the voice world, and I am a huge fan. I recommend her courses for anyone who wants to understand the voice and vocal tract function on a higher level. She is also a gifted voice rehabilitation expert, and I recommend her highly if you have been referred to a speech-language pathologist for any vocal issues or injuries. obertvoicestudios.com

Dr. Ian Howell is a singer, educator, and researcher who is leading the way in understanding vocal tract resonances. His theory of

Absolute Spectral Tone Color was a game-changer for my teaching and understanding of the voice. embodiedmusiclab.com

Carole D'Andrea is a gifted and respected acting teacher who also coaches singers to bring out the emotion in song. Carole is available for online distance learning. caroledandrea@gmail.com

# ENTs

I have worked with and highly recommend the following ENTs who are all deeply experienced in working with singers. They are also available for telehealth and second opinions.

Dr. Reena Gupta. centerforvocalhealth.com

Dr. Curt Stock. mountainwestent.com/drstock

Dr. H. Steven Sims chicagovoicedoc.com

## NCVS Prescriptions Side Effects Chart

Want to know how a medication will affect your voice? This is the best online resource I have found. NCVS is a leading research institution for singers and high-level voice users.

https://ncvs.org/prescriptions/

## Where to Find Me

The Intelligent Vocalist is my weekly podcast that has listeners from around the world. I discuss singing, voice science, mindset, and more. I also bring in fantastic special guests. johnhenny.com/category/podcast/

VoiceSchool.com is where I help and interact with singers globally. Of all my projects, VoiceSchool.com is what I am most proud of.

# ACKNOWLEDGMENTS

Eric Futterer: Eric was my first voice teacher and took me from a drummer to a lead vocalist with a record deal. His encouragement and expertise changed my life.

Seth Riggs: This legend and iconoclast is still going strong in his nineties. Seth has taught more legendary singers than anyone before or since. Seth pushed me to teach and I never looked back.

Michael Goodrich: Michael Goodrich is a mentor/teacher who encouraged me to create online courses. I have met so many great students because of Michael's influence.

Kerrie Obert: I have mentioned Kerrie throughout this book. She helped save my voice and my career, and I am forever thankful for her presence in the vocal world.

Kenneth Bozeman: Ken Bozeman is a leading teacher in vocal acoustics who has helped me immeasurably with his generosity and kindness. He is a beacon of the voice community, and his work enriches us all.

Ian Howell: At some point, all voice teachers need to know Ian's work. His understanding of vowels changed my teaching, and my students are the better for it.

Jeremy Ryan Mossman: Jeremy is a wonderfully free thinker whos work is instrumental in helping singers and teachers understand fascia and how it affects the voice.

Jeff Alani Stanfill: Jeff is a dear friend and brilliant voice teacher who helped me rediscover my voice as I was dealing with my vocal crisis.

Jaime Vendera: Jaime is the first person to encourage me to write a book, and I am forever thankful he did. Jaime is an all-around excellent voice teacher, but he is most well-known for teaching extreme scream styles and his ability to shatter glass with his voice (no joke!). Jaime's high screams can shake a room (and scare everyone in the vicinity), but he remains humble, warm, and someone you enjoy spending time with.

Tracee Theisen-Henny: The fact that you are reading this is a testament to my wife's tenacity and patience. Tracee pushes me into my office and sets deadlines whenever I start to whine about how hard it is to write a book (it's a lot).

And finally, you, the reader. Your time and attention are precious, and I appreciate you spending some of it with me and my ideas. I don't know you personally, but I have been thinking of and envisioning you in every moment spent writing this book. I am grateful for you and look forward to meeting or working with you someday.

# WHAT DID YOU THINK?

want to thank you for reading *The Mature Singer's Guidebook*.
I hope this book is a continuing resource for you and your singing.
   May I ask you a quick favor?

   If you found this book helpful, please consider leaving a review on Amazon.

   Reviews do make a difference in helping others find this book.

   To leave a review, head over to the Amazon page where you purchased '*The Mature Singer's Guidebook*'" and click on 'Write a customer review'.

   I also welcome your feedback at john@johnhenny.com

Thank you.
John Henny

# ABOUT THE AUTHOR

John Henny has decades of experience helping thousands of voice users around the world become more effective communicators.

He is a featured lecturer at top voice conferences and institutions, including IVTOM, Osborne Head and Neck Institute, VIP Worldwide Voice Conference, The Paul McCartney Liverpool Institute and USC.

John is the author of four Amazon bestselling books, hosts the popular podcast The Intelligent Vocalist and his YouTube channel has well over 100,000 subscribers.

# ALSO BY JOHN HENNY

*Beginning Singing: Expand Your Range, Improve Your Tone, and Create a Voice You'll Love*

*Teaching Contemporary Singing: The Proven Method for Becoming a Successful, Confident Voice Teacher, and Getting Vocal Breakthroughs for Your Students*

*The Compelling Speaker: How to Transform Your Voice for Maximum Impact, Persuasion, and Connection*

*Voice Teacher Influencer: Grow Your Studio, Increase Your Authority, and Make More Money*

Made in the USA
Monee, IL
24 November 2024

71057165R00072